TEACHING MEN TO BE FEMINIST

TEACHING MEN TO BE FEMINIST

ANNE DICKSON

QUARTET

First published in 2013 by Quartet Books Limited
A member of the Namara Group
27 Goodge Street, London W1T 2LD
Copyright © Anne Dickson 2013
The right of Anne Dickson to be identified
as the author of this work has been asserted
by her in accordance with the
Copyright, Designs and Patents Act, 1988
A catalogue record for this book
is available from the British Library
ISBN 978 0 7043 7340 2
Typeset by Josh Bryson
Printed and bound in Great Britain by
T J International Ltd, Padstow, Cornwall

CONTENTS

CONTENTS

INTRODUCTION

One of the catalysts for this book was a discussion between various men on the radio earlier this year about the incidence of racism in football. Taking part were football pundits, players, coaches, referees and match supporters. I listened to these men using phrases like 'we should not tolerate racism in this day and age'; 'racism brings shame on the game for all of us' and 'we must adopt a zero tolerance approach to racism in all its forms'.

It is important obviously to raise awareness about racism but it strikes me as unimaginable that I would ever hear a miscellany of male voices protesting about *sex*ism. Apart from party political statements every now and then promising to tackle problems of inequality when wooing prospective female voters, I hear nothing. I have never personally heard a man protest about sexism – only women, and even then relatively few. So if ordinary guys can speak with such conviction about racism, what gets in the way of a similar conviction about sexism?

A cynical response would be that men have too much to lose by challenging sexism because they are the ones with the power: benefits of power are always harder to release than to fight for. There is some truth in this but there are additional, more subtle factors at play: most men think feminism is about equal pay and equal rights and equal access for women to top positions of power. Very few people seem to understand what sexism is, how it operates and the intense damage it does: unlike racism, you can't always see when it's operating.

I have long been puzzled by men's lack of endorsement of feminism. What goes through a man's mind when he fears for his daughter's safety or hears her playing down her intelligence in front of her boyfriend? Why does a man keep silent when he sees a female colleague being bullied or when he knows a woman has lost out unfairly to a male colleague regarding promotion despite her evident competence? How does a man feel when his partner becomes utterly distraught by an extra centimetre she has gained around her waist? Do men ever think beyond the individual instance to try and understand the way the system of sexism functions? Do men really care about such things?

One obstacle is a generalised resentment, some of it well-founded. The advancement of several women up the ranks is not seen unequivocally as 'a good thing'. I hear men (and women) lament the loss of what they regard as femininity, uncomfortable with the changes they see in women's behaviour: how much more uppity they are, more in your face, more grasping, more outspoken and even more ruthless than men. This resentment is stoked by the popular media which steadily feeds us titbits about the woman who claims to have been harassed or even raped without any foundation or about the ex-wife who uses the weight of the law to exact revenge on a rejecting husband by extracting every bit of money she can from his coffers, intent on fleecing him as punishment for having spurned her.

If men in a culture like our own think at all about sexism today, I believe they imagine sexism refers to the glaring inequities between what men and women are permitted to do in other parts of the world. This can lead to a complacency which insists that over *here*, equality has long been established so women have nothing more to be feminist about. For me, this leads directly to two major problems.

First, unlike racism, the box relating to sexism has in many people's minds been ticked as if it's no longer an issue. Secondly, again unlike racism, challenging sexism in the past and even if mentioned today has been and still is considered to be a *woman*'s thing like lipstick or lingerie.

This book is an attempt to challenge these particular assumptions by showing how sexism affects us all, damages us all and why feminism is still key to changing this. I am, of course, aware that in many cultures and countries, including my own, many of those upholding patriarchal structures remain and intend to remain completely unreflective about sexist attitudes and behaviour. I do not intend therefore to waste my energy on trying to convert anyone, so who is this book aimed at?

It is for any man who feels excluded by feminism, who believes it is a manifesto whereby women ultimately take over the reins of power leaving men emasculated. It is for men who believe that feminism so far has only produced ballbreakers who make life hell for everyone around them. It is a deliberate attempt, on my part, to reach out to the kind of men who are often deeply interested in what I have to say and teach or write about but hesitate to admit it; to those men who sense the injustice and inequality of sexism but shrink from making any comment. Many younger men emerging from a cultural focus on individual rights are baffled by hostile opposition to gender equality: to them everyone should have equal rights, end of story. But disagreeing with something in principle can lead to a certain blindness regarding the continuing realities of sexism, so I am writing for these men too.

It is for those men who already question the status quo, who are sometimes doubtful about their own masculine role and feel they have to tread on eggshells when relating to women in the midst of a sea change in gender stereotypes and expectations. It is for men who, for example, find themselves hesitating or confused sometimes about who should pay on a first date, who should cook the meal, who should take what initiative. How do you juggle the need to avoid looking old-fashioned and quaint while also making the right impression?

I am writing for men who find themselves believing there is some truth in the frequently heard rationalisation that a female rape victim was 'asking for it' by getting drunk or dressing provocatively although they would never acknowledge this out loud. This book is also an attempt to reach out to those men I have met and spoken to who feel deeply alienated by the current structures of power in the world and yearn for other values, for other qualities in life; who hate the materialism of our world but who do not see any clear alternatives.

I hope it will be read by men who love their partners and daughters and do not want to see them hurt or treated unfairly but cannot find a way to speak up when they perceive sexism in action because, being men themselves, they feel too uncomfortable and helpless to do so. I am writing for any man who would like to feel more human, who would perhaps like to explore some of these issues without it feeling as threatening or as potentially explosive as walking through a minefield.

As a system, sexism could not have continued for as long as it has without women's active *and* passive collusion, a fact that easily gets overlooked. Most of what I have written in the past has been aimed at women as an extension of my teaching and training, always with the purpose of facilitating more emotional independence and thus more confidence in challenging the status quo. Despite some success, the unthinking habit of sexism in everyday life takes its toll: we are all born into a world where both genders share a legacy of sexist brainwashing. While I believe women are especially adversely affected by this legacy, I want to explain how and why, for different reasons, we all contribute to the maintenance of the same system which may be as revealing and discomforting for women as well as men. It's only when we all recognise the games we play that we have the possibility of other options.

This book is not an easy read because the subject matter hardly constitutes a walk in the park; it has certainly taken me to some dark places while engaged in writing it. However, my hope is that with more understanding and more care we can begin to have a new conversation and move forward *together*.

1
SEXISM AND FEMINISM: THE BASICS

Feminism is an ideological challenge to sexism, for some men perhaps conjuring up immediate associations of militancy and hostility towards all those of the male gender. Older men may recall images of 'liberated' women burning their bras in symbolic protest against oppression while younger men (and many young women) continue to assume that any pro-feminist action is by definition *anti*-men.

There have been many attempts to trivialise feminism: trivialisation of all oppressive structures not only ignores entire histories of suffering but also conveniently misses the point. I remember, for instance, the announcement around twenty-five years ago that the north London borough in which I then lived had decided to replace the black bags distributed to householders for years with pink ones. Why? The official explanation was that, in increasingly politically correct times, using black bags risked insinuating that people of colour were associated with rubbish. I groaned inwardly at the time much as I do when a man refuses to hold a door open while I'm struggling to get through with a heavy case, because a woman can't expect to be feminist and, so I've been told, be treated like a lady!

If feminism is a challenge to sexism, then what exactly is sexism? A simple definition is discrimination against a person on account of their gender. Although both men and women can be subject to this form of bias, my current focus is on discrimination against women.

Sexism exists as a conscious and unconscious ideology. Like racism, ageism, heterosexism, fascism and so on, the ideology of sexism establishes a demarcation of power designating who is above and who is below in the pecking order; who should have more say, more sway and more access to whatever social goods are available.

There is a pervasive belief currently in this post-modern world that sexism is an exaggerated and now outdated oppression dreamed up by a few women in the past who felt aggrieved about being excluded from voting or from access to certain professions. So much has changed for the better that it has become less fashionable these days to talk of inequality; sexism – and therefore by implication feminism – is something that belongs to the past like writing letters or family meals shared together round a table. Men's eyes tend to glaze over when the subject is raised and most women look faintly embarrassed.

Many claim 'Times have changed' and that 'Young men and women are completely different from the past generation'. Even when evidence of sexism rears its ugly head in the media every now and then, its impact is offset by payment of vast sums in compensation for sexual harassment or discrimination so it's easy to be sceptical and conclude that women are hardly 'disadvantaged' any more.

SEXISM AND FEMINISM

After a public talk I gave last year, I was told by a Danish friend who had listened to me that I had been brave to acknowledge I was a feminist because it was not something women in her own country would openly assert these days. It's hard for me to understand how we can dismiss feminist protest as fighting a war that is past history when sexism is very much alive and kicking in 2013.

In terms of ideological impact, the unequal repercussions of sexism are universal. A casual glance at the ladders of power in every country and every nationality in the world reveal that women on the higher echelons of hierarchical power are the exception. This applies to positions in government, corporate, industrial, commercial, academic, medical, financial and religious institutions, the armed forces and the civil service. A search through the hallowed halls of revered composers, scientists, painters, inventors, sculptors, explorers, architects, philosophers or poets – past and present – will disclose the same phenomenon.

Very often the exceptions to this norm – those famous and infamous women who have made it onto higher rungs or ruled nations for a while – are cited to forestall any potential protest. The problem is that these particular women often appear so cold, fearsome or corrupt that they do not offer valuable or positive role models.

So how do we explain the remarkable absence of the female gender? What puts men higher up the ladder? What keeps them there? How come that being born with testicles means that you are automatically placed on a higher rung than being born without? Is it that women are inferior in some way, perhaps less intelligent, less hardworking, less competent or less enduring? Is women's role in the world better served elsewhere?

Would women really achieve a greater sense of fulfilment if they were more equally represented in the higher strata of power? Does gender inequality actually *matter*? These questions and their repercussions on our lives have been discussed by women and men for over hundreds of years. Millions of words, and years of time and energy, have been dedicated to challenge and counter challenge. Protagonists of feminism have encouraged women to move upwards, each gain marking a higher rung on the ladder and the past one hundred and fifty years have seen a huge change in women's status throughout much of the world. Many young women today take for granted rights that were not available to their mothers and that their grandmothers could only have dreamed of.

The conclusion that sexism (and by implication feminism) belongs to a different era is influenced by the higher public profile of women in positions of authority, usually in business or in government. This has had a different effect from seeing women who are powerful through wealth or beauty because now women hold visible positions of legitimate power over others. However, thinking that women have 'the same opportunities' as men now is more wishful than reality-based thinking. Simply because an occasional woman appears on (or near) the top rung of her professional ladder and a smattering of women are promoted to senior managerial or executive positions, we don't comment very loudly on the remaining imbalance or absence of women from the highest echelons. Is it because now women believe they're finally getting somewhere, they don't like to draw attention to the down side? It doesn't seem as newsworthy any more or worth questioning, as though previous grievances have been attributed to a problem of mere mismanagement that has now been addressed and corrected, once and for all.

Certainly, legal enshrinement of equal pay structures in many countries in the Western world is to some extent indicative of improvement but this doesn't actually mean equal in real terms. Inequality has different manifestations according to specific cultural, historical and social factors. In the UK, female remuneration in the UK is currently around seventy per cent of what men earn in an equivalent job. Women in Saudi Arabia are forbidden from driving cars; women in sub-Saharan Africa or Southern Asia are denied rights to owning any land. In Japan, women must use a linguistic prefix when speaking: asking for a glass of water, for example, changes depending on whether a man or a woman is speaking to comply with the difference in gender status. These are only a few of many examples but differential treatment is always based on one basic premise: they are *women*. No further explanation is necessary.

Despite ample evidence of remaining inequality it is nevertheless misleading to reduce sexism to a list of symptoms. If we really want to understand how it operates and to understand the harm inflicted by sexist ideology, we have to dig deeper to uncover an all-encompassing mindset, perpetuated by attitudes and behaviour based on assumptions about gender which constitute the entire fabric of our lives.

2
A PATRIARCHAL PROFILE

It is often argued that male and female genders have innately different capabilities and aptitudes. I'm often intrigued myself that people who are explorers, jazz instrumentalists, undertakers, railway enthusiasts, anglers, engineers, twitchers, footballers, racing car enthusiasts and hackers are overwhelmingly if not exclusively male in gender. Is this due to different capabilities genetically or conditioning through contrasting opportunities and encouragement? Or both?

In normal circumstances we assume a greater physical strength in the male of the human species (even allowing for individual development and variation) as well as a higher average body temperature. Colour blindness is carried by a male gene so only affects men. Women, on the other hand, tend to have a different spatial awareness and weaker livers so are more vulnerable than men to the effects of alcohol but otherwise tend to outlive them. However, these and other phenomena don't matter so much here: sexism goes way beyond a question of *vive la différence*.

Gender difference and gender discrimination are not the same. Gender difference explains some of our biological and possibly emotional variations according to stereotypical profiles. Gender discrimination is not a question of difference (different but equal) but of a *weighted* difference in the sense that one gender (and every attribute associated with that gender) is more valued, more prized, more respected, more desired than the other. Difference is no longer a question of variety but a question of hierarchy. As soon as you create a hierarchical distinction, you have a definition of gender difference that is forever *unequal*. Sexism refers to the subtle but ingrained assumption of the superiority of one of those two genders. It is always a question of one *over* the other. There is not a single area in life that has not been influenced by this assumption. Not one.

This sounds simple but it is extraordinary how we live with and by this core belief from birth to death, often never questioning its basis any more than we think of analysing the way we put one foot in front of the other when we walk.

The Body Politic

The patriarchical destiny of any human being is mapped out from birth: if you're born into a female body, you're automatically ascribed an inferior status. What's so distinctive about a woman's body? The body of the female human species tends to be physically weaker than that of the male; increased oestrogen levels mean there is more fatty tissue and softer muscle tone; women naturally experience monthly cycles of bleeding and physiological/ emotional changes in relation to these hormonal cycles.

14

In addition, sexual arousal and release in the female is a hidden, internal process with no clear and obvious demarcation of different stages of the cycle. Compare this with the genitals of the male: visible on the outside, obvious in all stages of sexual arousal and with clear indications of sexual release.

Natural childbirth is a messy affair: physical pain is involved and female reproductive paraphernalia is hidden, remaining a little mysterious but, crucially, extremely powerful. The ability to conceive, gestate and give birth to new life, after all, pretty much tops any creative undertaking men's bodies have ever been able to engage in – really no competition at all. So it's not hard to imagine that, in the dim and distant past, the combination of mystery and awe seasoned with a massive pinch of envy could have fuelled early cavemen's stereotypical treatment of early cavewomen as their underlings and inferiors. What else could they do to maintain credibility in the face of such an extraordinary, superhuman ability?

The foundation and establishment of patriarchy over time provided a means of ensuring that henceforth men could rule over women; that they would make the important decisions; that property and wealth would be handed down through the males in the family; that important positions be held by men; and that women correspondingly should treat *them* as superior. Quite an extraordinary turnaround really: to persuade women that despite their awesome reproductive capacities, their bodies were mere receptacles for the god-like seed.

I have come to regard sexism as the most widespread and effective process of brainwashing in the history of humankind, carried out and maintained by every single kind of institution run by men, for men, thinking like men and establishing their own kind of values based on their own aims and ambitions, sometimes benign, often not. Every single structure of daily life – legal, social, institutional, political, cultural, religious – has been and still is organised around unequal gender assumptions.

One of the most influential of these institutions has undoubtedly been the church, through the teaching of religious doctrines in most parts of the world. There are few religious faiths which do not teach that women are spiritually inferior so that, correspondingly, they must take a lower place in the scheme of things, both religious and secular. Women must worship separately or at least be denied access to a position in an ecclesiastic hierarchy that has been designated (and should continue) as the exclusive domain of those of the superior gender.

Have you ever asked yourself why this is? Why is it that women should not be afforded equal status within most religions? You may never have met or known a woman who wanted to serve her community as a bishop or who wanted to pray within the body of a church instead of on the sidelines but have you ever wondered what the basis was for this manifest hostility towards equality in religious spheres? Even if you're not personally interested in religion, understanding this connection reveals something quite extraordinary.

A PATRIARCHAL PROFILE

The spiritual injunction is of particular significance because it is most profoundly rooted in the belief that a woman's body is less clean than a man's body. Why? Putting it simply, because she bleeds. This is not a Western invention: from Judaism to Jainism, Christianity to Islam, a woman's very *femaleness* is equated with her spiritual inequality. Whether the particular emphasis is on impurity related to various myths about blood loss or the inherently dangerous capacity of a woman to corrupt and seduce men towards earthly rather than heavenly joys, the jaw-dropping reality is the persistence of these beliefs precisely because they have been around for so long. They are embedded within the histories and traditions of many cultures: of course, it is only a short 'logical' step from a woman's intrinsic spiritual inferiority to her intrinsic status as a second-class citizen in every other respect.

Past and current attitudes of male clerics in many religions towards the place of women can be reasoned out and 'justified' with ample references to religious texts or to the gender of the supreme divine being Himself. Ultimately, though, any theological underpinning to the idea of treating women as spiritual equals masks the deeper, hidden bedrock obstruction which is the undying belief that women are 'unclean' and, by definition, spiritually inferior.

And if you think this belongs to a past era, consider that earlier this year a group of Jewish women, trying to assert their equal right to pray at the Holy Wall in Jerusalem, were attacked with rocks for daring to protest about their exclusion. In November 2012, after lengthy deliberations, the Church of England finally decided against giving women the right to be ordained as bishops.

Even when women are accepted into religious orders, their status is regarded as subservient. Also last year, after spending their lives serving the underprivileged in society, a council of Catholic nuns in the US began to question openly their church's prohibitions on women serving as priests, birth control and the rejection of same-sex relationships. This resulted in a severe reproof from the Vatican on account of their 'excessively feminist attitudes' with a threat to take away their autonomy and place them under the pastoral guidance of a bishop. And if you are unlucky enough to be born with female genitals in Somalia, despite a law in the country banning the practice, you're likely to be one of the ninety-six per cent of women there who have been subjected to clitoridectomy according to the requirements of local Islamic tradition.

Today many women all over the world face a daily conflict with the legacy of sexism in their chosen religious faiths. Unless one can grasp the truly extraordinary *power* of the assumption that a woman's body is essentially impure, one can never comprehend the undying hold that sexism has on the world's population. The increase of secular lifestyles in the West and the decline in religious affiliation does nothing to alter this belief. Whether a woman is applying for a job as a stockbroker or bishop, she will be subject to sexist attitudes which deep down can be found to have common roots: the inferiority of her body. Despite our politically correct times, it doesn't take more than a little scratch across the veneer of 'we are genuinely committed to gender equality' to reveal these kind of attitudes and, what's more, the deep loathing which fuels opposition to change in this regard.

Although Sigmund Freud didn't help with the huge influence of his description of 'vagina dentata', he does not account singlehandedly for the ubiquitous negativity towards female genitals which continues today in a plethora of forms: from female circumcision to the pressure to shave every inch of natural pubic hair or to have vaginal plastic surgery to emulate the norms of clean, hairless, trim and symmetrical labia featured in close-up porn shots. This is the (male) ideal – making something (naturally) repulsive into something that is sexually stimulating.

Has the ideology of feminism managed to shift the cultural negativity towards female genitalia? Do today's young women celebrate and rejoice in their own genitals when affirming their sexuality? On a recent visit to a women's sex shop in London (for young women run by young women) I couldn't help noticing that among two entire floors of sexual images, toys, gadgets, clothes, props and general sexual paraphernalia, the only visible genital representations – and there were many of them in a variety of forms – were male. There were cocks in pots, like geraniums, in the form of candles and dildos or pictured on walls. It was difficult not to conclude that modern women, asserting their equal rights to sexual pleasure – a fundamentally laudable aim – could only achieve this by associating woman's sexual power with (and over) male genitals. My search revealed one exception: hidden at the back of a shelf was a tiny embroidered cotton vulva on sale as a glove puppet.

For many years I facilitated sexuality groups for women, specifically to address this shroud of negativity. One major 'homework' assignment in the programme meant each woman had the task of looking at her genitals in a mirror at home. Every single time, women disclosed their responses of complete unfamiliarity at best and revulsion at worst: associations of ugliness, imperfections, absent or negative terminology, revilement and rejection. Slowly and with support, curiosity led to familiarity and for many, even to affirmation and reconnection with this hidden fragment of their bodies. I realise a man can often be concerned about the size or shape of his penis, but what I am describing is a response to a key part of our bodies that is one of ignorance, alienation and even shame.

There are other spin-offs to the myths of a woman's 'evil' body: the absence of female genitals in many representations in Western art especially, for example, and the transformation of the word 'cunt'. This was once a perfectly ordinary word associated with shrewdness and wisdom – but over centuries of sexism, it has evolved to its modern usage as the word chosen to revile someone in the *worst* possible way. Unlike 'dick' or 'cock', 'cunt' is never used in jest or to imply mere stupidity: it is a vehicle of utter contempt. Another instance of the achievements of sexist brainwashing.

3
THE DYNAMICS OF DOMINATION

How has patriarchal thinking become the only way of thinking? Patriarchal structures go back such a long time that we cannot find any frame of reference as an alternative. Archaeological discoveries offer strong evidence of the existence for over thirty thousand years of matriarchal societies which continued up to somewhere between 3000 and 4000 BC. Feminists have understood, correctly in my opinion, that such evidence points to the indisputable fact that patriarchy has been *imposed* on us – i.e. it does not represent the natural way of things between the sexes but is a culturally constructed fiction.

This is what is important for the purposes of this book – not the relative benefits of matriarchy and patriarchy (although there is evidence that women fared better under matriarchal cultures), but if you as a reader can grasp that patriarchy, and therefore sexism, is not part of a genetic but a cultural heritage, then you can open an important door to understanding patriarchy as one particular system. A highly effective system, in many ways, but nevertheless constructed and therefore *not* the inevitable or natural lot of humanity.

So what makes one group dominant over another? Is it larger? Not necessarily. Nor is it necessarily better armed, more advanced, more resourceful or better organised. What is essential, though, to the dynamic of the relationship is that the dominant group *assumes* superiority. This means it operates on an assumption that such superiority is unquestionable, 'god-given' or part of the natural and fixed (hierarchical) order of things.

The complementary assumption is the natural or 'god-given' inferiority of the lower group. In the course of history, this inferiority has been labelled heathen, godless, primitive, under-developed, quaint, backward, naïve or even cute but it always designates a group which is ultimately branded as inferior.

How does one culture become dominant over another? The dynamic of domination – between individuals, groups or nations – tends to follow the same pattern in that there is always a two-way relationship. Every dominant group has to have a lower group over which it can dominate: it stands to reason you cannot dominate if you have nothing to dominate over any more than you can win if there is nobody to lose. These dynamics can be seen in many examples of lower groups, both historically and currently: black Americans, peasants, native American Indians, working classes, the poor, Irish, mulattos, Serbs, lower castes, Jews, the mentally or physically disabled, Aborigines, Incas, Tibetans, Afro-Caribbeans and gypsies. Each of these has experienced – and in some instances continues to experience – being oppressed by a dominant group.

To maintain dominance, the culture of the lower group must be defined and treated as inferior. The word 'culture' describes a frame of reference for shared beliefs about the meaning of life, from birth to death and everything in between. Any people's culture embraces code of dress, values, rituals, social and domestic practices and the complex structures of social, family and national life. It also includes language, music, literature, art, food and customs. Culture describes how we see ourselves in relation to each other and to the world around us.

Whatever the culture of the lower group, the dominant group demands that it be, at its most benevolent, superimposed or at its most violent, exterminated through the process of colonisation. When this happens the 'colonised' group loses its own culture. A new language is imposed; a new dress code; new social practices; new diet; a new god; a new way of life which constitutes a whole new 'culture'. The original culture of the lower group now becomes *muted* by the dominance of the other.

Historically, it is interesting to note that many cultures that have become muted through colonisation were not built around patriarchal beliefs; for example, the Maoris, Native American Indians and Aboriginal peoples. Sometimes a muted culture goes underground: a language, religious practice or social custom is kept alive, secretly, to avoid sanctions by the dominant group but, more often, these cultures die out and are lost forever.

Once any dominant group is in power, how does it stay there? It needs to gain access, by force if necessary, to all other facets of hierarchical power: resources, wealth, information, expertise, governmental or military control.

Then the dominant group has to hold on tightly to these forms of power by any means which it can claim to 'justify' this end. Unsurprisingly, justification is always found.

It takes a bit of an imaginative leap to see how the dominant/muted dynamic relates to gender. Although we cannot point to one moment in history when women were colonised by men, the assumed superiority of the male over the female gender is easily recognisable. There appears to be some general consensus about certain influential factors among experts who have studied this phenomenon: the shift from the hunter-gatherer way of life to agricultural cultivation which necessitated marking of territorial boundaries. The establishment of ownership of territory gave rise to the subsequent need for aggressive defence of it. Archaeologists have long believed that war has been the impetus behind the process of civilisation. It is generally accepted that the need to band together to fight a common enemy produced the transition from small, autonomous, self-governing and self-sustaining communities to a much larger population governed by hierarchical rule. Aggression, in all its forms, has been an intrinsic part of an up/down system as far back as we can remember.

A further historical factor was the evolution from the polytheistic structure of goddess-centred worship of matriarchal societies to the monotheism of Christianity and Islam (preceded by Judaism) which date back to 2000 BC. This development added impetus to hierarchy and patriarchy.

I cannot begin to do justice to these matters. What I know is that despite ongoing academic debates, there is irrefutable evidence that at some point in our history, patriarchal beliefs did not dominate. Right now, my question is more concerned with understanding how on earth we have arrived in the year 2013 with relations between the sexes still largely determined by the same patriarchally-formulated inequality as four thousand years ago.

It is certainly not because there has been no protest. For the last two hundred years (and even before) sexism has been challenged over and over again by many female literary giants (Mary Wollstonecraft, Simone de Beauvoir and Germaine Greer among many) citing indisputable and overwhelming evidence of the effect of patriarchy on women. Millions of words have been written in both populist and academic form, but still the power play of men over women continues on and on. We have become so accustomed to it that we believe it's normal.

4
THE ACCEPTABLE FACE
OF SEXISM

The acceptable face of sexism is how I describe the aspects of sexism we – men and women – take for granted: the everyday manifestations that elicit no more than a grimace or shrug from most women and are barely noticed by most men. These apparently insignificant occurrences are habitual both in the behaviour itself and the responses to that behaviour: this is what makes them seem so 'normal'.

In recent media coverage of one man after another implicated in the predatory pursuits which occurred throughout Jimmy Savile's career as a television presenter, there has been frequent reference to 'the culture' of the institution quoting comments from women who were working there at the time along the lines of, 'That's what it was like in those days…you simply got used to it.' Women do get used to it.

I once asked a female audience attending a lecture to indicate whether they had ever been on the receiving end of sexual harassment during their lives: harassment included being flashed at, unwanted sexual comments or physical contact, assault, attempted or actual rape. Although this doesn't count as serious research, every woman in the room was astonished to see so many hands go up. There were only two exceptions out of the group of thirty-four women.

The majority of them hadn't ever discussed these issues: this is what life is like. The culture within the BBC reflects the culture at large: women become habituated. For many of us, it is all we have ever known.

There is also a tendency to dismiss this phenomenon as belonging to the bad old days and to assure everyone that nothing like that could happen today. This is not true. Twenty- and thirty-year-old women continue to be subject to unwanted attention in the form of comments and gropes in their working environment. They too get used to it.

Certainly, things have changed and overt sexist behaviour is less publically acceptable because it is now against the law; lewd remarks or lascivious innuendos in the office, pub or street have been toned down. But what happens when being grossly sexist becomes politically incorrect? Just because we're told it's no longer socially acceptable and that there may be a penalty to pay for transgression, sexism doesn't disappear; it goes underground instead. In the privacy of their own close friendships, many men share and enjoy sexist banter, aware that they continue to look at women as sexual objects, rating them mentally according to their personal 'fuckability' scale even if they keep their unarticulated fantasies firmly under wraps in women's company.

Despite – or perhaps because of – the shift to political correctness, most men indulge in 'closet' sexism. The majority, especially those in their younger years and who would regard themselves as quite laid back, still allow themselves some latitude in private. For most men, this latitude exists alongside a genuine abhorrence of any violence towards women.

Extreme behaviour is associated with hatred of women so it makes no sense to heterosexual males even if they are confused and uncertain about their own power position. Nevertheless the wide margin of acceptable sexism continues for the most part unchallenged. All of us close our eyes to many comments, attitudes, gestures and even evident prejudice because the ideology of sexism runs incredibly deep, layer upon layer built over the centuries, reinforced institutionally for so long that we cannot remember life any differently.

Reinforcement continues less consciously as well. Even when sexist banter is shared privately, it is shared consciously. The problem with the habit of sexism is that it influences us far beyond the conscious mind: much sexist behaviour is *unthinking* behaviour. It is this lack of thought or reflection which makes attitudes virtually impossible to shift. Knowingly curbing your sexist comments or actions is only possible when you become aware of them: most men – and indeed many women – are so mentally programmed by and accustomed to sexism that we never consider it optional. Habit blinds us to alternatives and the pervasive habit of sexism also blinds us to repercussions and implications of the patterns and connections *between* sexist behaviours.

Where and when and how does the acceptable face of sexism change to being considered unacceptable? I have tried to illustrate this question by looking at different manifestations of sexism as a continuum composed of examples of men's sexist behaviour and attitudes, beginning with what might be termed commonplace and therefore 'acceptable' and ending with the downright criminal.

THE ACCEPTABLE FACE OF SEXISM

- Prioritising suggestions made by men in a personal or professional context
- Blaming your son for not being more athletic or masculine
- Criticising your daughter for not being more attractive or more feminine
- Encouraging your daughter to be self-conscious about her appearance
- Overt or covert disapproval of a girl/woman who expresses anger
- Trivialising a woman's expression of her emotions as over-emotional or hysterical
- Privately attributing what you consider to be a woman's unacceptable behaviour to her hormones
- Taking for granted that a woman is always happy to provide you with an audience of one
- Subjecting women to a physical-appearance rating (mentally or verbally)
- Mistrusting intelligent women
- Using a woman's body as a sex object to sell publications, cars, alcohol or whatever
- Being an avowed hips/legs/tits man
- Turning a blind eye/deaf ear to sexist comments
- Using the word 'cunt' as a term of loathing
- Responding with humour to sexist exploits in friends/colleagues/bosses/employees
- Colluding with institutional silence about forms of sexism such as harassment, comments or unfair treatment of women in the workplace
- Firing a female employee for taking maternity leave
- Refusing promotion to (or otherwise penalising) a female employee who has young children
- Giving preferential treatment to a male over a female job applicant for no other reason than gender
- Favouring a female candidate on account of her appearance rather than ability

- Using the power of your professional role to elicit sexual favours
- Any form of emotional violence towards a woman, e.g. constant criticism or putdowns
- Refusing to consult with or give equal consideration to the needs/belief/wishes of your female partner
- Intolerance of any disagreement (by a woman) with your own decisions
- Insisting on the 'My word is the law' rule at home
- Controlling a woman's behaviour through sulking, menace or manipulation to get your own way
- Unsolicited touch anywhere on the body – arms, head, face, back, shoulders
- Unsolicited fondling of a woman's breasts, buttocks or thighs
- Commenting suggestively on a woman's physical appearance
- Making sexual innuendoes
- Looking/ogling/leering at a woman's body
- Masturbating to pornography which depicts violence towards women
- Intimidating a woman with an aggressive manner
- Threatening a woman with physical violence
- Using physical violence – pinching/prodding/slapping/biting/choking/hair-pulling/punching/ kicking – as a punishment for some misdemeanour or to show you're superior
- Manipulating or pressurising a woman into sexual activity when she is drunk
- Coercing a woman into continuing any kind of sexual activity when she is in any way hesitant or unwilling
- Rape
- Murder

THE ACCEPTABLE FACE OF SEXISM

This is a sample range of attitudes and behaviours which, woven together, constitute the fabric of sexist expression. Admittedly the range is arbitrary and the examples vary in terms of social or criminal severity but the common denominator is that each instance is predicated on *male power over the female*. This reveals an essential feature of sexism: it is all about power – who has it and who doesn't. Each one of these examples springs from exactly the same source: the aware *or* unaware wish to assert or maintain power over a woman's body and, by extension, her mind.

What interests me is where along the continuum does sexism become personally *un*acceptable for any individual man? Where does a man draw the line and why at that point particularly? Once we begin to see what constitutes the acceptable face of sexism, we uncover a widespread and habitual incidence of attitudes and actions which may appear entirely unremarkable in themselves. Small habits of sexism emerge all the time, every day, everywhere: rarely challenged and often not even noticed. This is because unthinking habits of sexism are acquired by being born male or female within a system in which one gender dominates over the other.

5
KNOWING OUR PLACE

Although I have presented a picture of sexist attitudes and behaviour from a male point of view, it would be incomplete without understanding where women fit into this picture. To understand this we have to go back to group dynamics again. What happens psychologically to any group which finds itself in the lower group, the one that is forever dominated by the superior? Understanding this is helpful when it comes to trying to grasp how women respond to sexism in the way that they do.

Within any system of colonisation, the members of the lower group internalise their inferiority. They may dislike it or may even hate it but they become convinced of it. Around the age of six, each of us learns where we belong: to a group of lower or upper status, whether in relation to gender, race, class, caste or even a disabled child among the able-bodied. Sexism is upheld and maintained by men and women together: we all grow up in a sexist system. Depending on individual personalities and life experience, we will uphold it, question it or learn to cope with it.

For any up/down system to be held in place, the dominant assumptions of superiority are only half the story: nothing could be held in place for long without the complementary assumptions of the lower group. The lower group must *believe* it is inferior or, at the very least, if not exactly inferior, there has to be sneaking suspicion that there must be some good reason why the status quo is as it is. Whether 'god-given' or simply the natural order of things, there must be a reason why and the easy, though mistaken conclusion is to assume that the fault lies within.

This assumption is born out of powerlessness to effect any change. The muted group tends to internalise this imposed 'natural' order in order to survive; in other words, the longer it lasts, the more often revolution fails and the status quo restored, the more deeply etched in the psyche of the 'inferior' group is the acceptance of its inequality. Individuals in the muted group may respond with acquiescence or anger, submission or protest, but eventually, and to some degree unconsciously, they absorb the message.

The superior/inferior gender demarcation has a profound effect. Some women embrace their role with huge enthusiasm and commitment, aiming to conform to the ideal in every way: pleasing men in appearance and behaviour as they know they should. Others rebel against the imposition and attempt to break out of the mould. Most women struggle along the way both colluding and protesting at different times in life, but it remains a fairly constant awareness. There are myriad habitual (and again unthinking) ways in which a woman can collude with sexism. Here are some examples:

- Automatically giving more credence to a man's statement than a woman's
- Educating her daughter to be feminine/pleasing/attractive/to hide her intelligence or her anger
- Prioritising a male guest/colleague/friend over female simply because he's male
- Refusing to challenge her son about sexist attitudes or behaviour
- Competing with other women to be the one who gets a particular man
- Encouraging a man to cheat on his wife
- Being profoundly thankful God is a man
- Disappointment at giving birth to a daughter rather than a son
- Joining in disapproval of a woman who is assertive or stands up for herself
- Condemning another woman's physical 'flaws' ('Did you see those wrinkles?'/'She has to be a dyke')
- Deliberately seducing another woman's husband/partner/boyfriend
- Refraining from justified criticism of a man, being reluctant to damage his male ego
- Letting a man think that what she wanted was actually his idea
- Dropping all her women friends when a new man comes on the scene
- Making light of a man's aggression/intimidation of another woman
- Suspecting women bring sexual violence on themselves
- Playing the helpless little girl in need of rescue
- Smiling indulgently at sexist banter
- Deliberately down-playing her (superior) knowledge of a particular issue in male company
- Treating adult men like little boys
- Categorising stay-at-home fathers at the school gates as distinctly unsexy

- Being convinced that she will lose sexually viability if there is no current man around to vouch for it
- Going along with sexual activity when she really doesn't want to
- Pretending to give a man undying attention (even when she stopped listening ages ago)
- Allowing her voice/opinions/feelings/wishes to be repeatedly over-ruled and silenced
- Going to any lengths to hold on to the man in her life rather than risk being alone
- Sneering at another woman's vulnerability or mistakes
- Refusing to help women lower down the ladder when she herself is in a position of power
- Being less forgiving about the faults of a female boss because she is a woman
- Turning a blind eye to harassment (or worse) of her daughter

I want to re-emphasise that a lot of this behaviour is unthinking; women can and do operate from a psychological premise, predicated on the gender hierarchy, which becomes so ingrained that they no longer bother to question the premise. Women have a long history of passive collusion, if not active endorsement: absence of challenge, failure to confront, keeping quiet, toeing the line and conforming to a prescribed standard of behaviour.

Sometimes this stems from a position of choice: women consciously decide to leave a situation or keep quiet because instinct warns that the need for self-preservation would best be served by doing so. Most of the time, however, passive collusion stems from a deep-rooted insecurity connected to an equally deep-rooted dependence on those in the higher position.

Whether we like it or not, there *is* a dominant system in place. It is a system we have in common but experience differently. There are other factors that affect our experience – class, wealth, education – but the bottom line is gender.

Whether we are born with or without testicles will determine the dynamic of our relationship to patriarchy, as clearly as the colour of skin determined a person's position in the system of apartheid. Whether a woman grows up in the body of a young girl in Saudi Arabia, Hungary, Afghanistan, Britain, France, Africa, China, India or South America, she'll soon understand her place in the grand scheme of things.

Gender affects our response most fundamentally whether we uphold the system, challenge it, benefit from it or fight to overturn it. We see a system in place and both men and women see men at the top. From a woman's point of view (looking upwards) this means that there is often something about a compliment, advice, approval or disapproval from a man – boss, father, lover, colleague – that has a more significant (higher) value: it somehow matters *more*.

Women may wear the trousers now, study construction engineering and initiate sex but, despite any feminist advances of the past one hundred years, the majority of women still feel dreadfully incomplete without a man. Women are rarely conscious of this higher value but it seeps into perceptions and responses.

It affects the way women see other women too. Mistrust often erodes co-operation, loyalty and lasting collaboration between women. This is not because women are untrustworthy but, as part of the lower group, women are lifetime competitors for the same prizes of male approval, acceptance and suitable (or even unsuitable) husbands. Women compete for all the dimensions of status predetermined within the dominant culture: appearance, body shape, intelligence, attractiveness, articulacy, marital status, mothering skill, sexiness or personality. At work women can add competence, status, salary and position which all apply to men as well except, between women, there is an extra edge to competition because top positions are far fewer.

Wariness of other women as potential competitors is almost like a default position; men, on the other hand, seem more straightforward and direct and, even though this can be a bit predictable, you know where you are whereas with women you're never sure. Even gay male friends are often more valued than women friends. A stumbling block to women's relationships with other women is that the image reflected back is a reminder of the common (inferior) status so that particular aptitudes and associations of femaleness become questionable and devalued.

Once you begin to understand how sexism works, it becomes possible to explain some puzzling phenomena. Why does research show that so many women suffer from clinical anxiety and depression? Why do women submit to expensive/time-consuming/painful treatments in order to be attractive? Why do so many women, for example, wear the highest of heels despite back pain and fatigue in the short-term and risk of spinal damage in the future? Why do women seek out cosmetic surgery without any man encouraging them to do so? Why do women stay in abusive relationships? We tend to see these as separate issues rather than making connections to sexism as the fundamental reference point.

What makes a psychological transition from sexism to feminism possible? Whatever the precise circumstances, the answer involves a process of acquiring consciousness. Precisely because so much of sexism is unconscious, it is only when it becomes conscious that we can begin to see a different reality. We begin to open our eyes to see that what appeared before as a given – the norm – is actually open to question. It can be a revelation to discover that patriarchy reflects a means of social conditioning: a very old, deeply entrenched and universal conditioning but, nonetheless, not representative of a *natural* state of affairs.

6
WOMAN'S BODY AS OBJECT

Feminists often refer to the damage caused to women by objectifying their bodies. What does this actually mean and why is it so important? An object, any object, is a thing like a boat, a hat or a banana. Each object has certain qualities we associate with it. If objects are inanimate we are happy to treat them as such but evidence of feelings or intelligence can give us pause for thought. Animals, for example, give rise to ambiguity. In our own culture, while people who love their pets see much more than an object, we are generally happy to treat cows, pigs and chickens as objects which can be reared in 'cost-effective' conditions, slaughtered and served up in a palatable form on our plates.

What about human beings? How do we mentally process a person into a thing? Before we can treat humans as objects, even useful, hardworking or desirable objects, they first have to be defined in our minds as objects. This means cutting out any awareness of an *inner existence*. An object has nothing abiding within, no permanent qualities unique to itself, no choice, no voice, no subjecthood. It becomes a thing, not a self. We develop blindness to the *whole* person and see only what we want to see.

This same psychological process occurs whether purchasing a slave to work as a beast of burden, sending a soldier to war, using a child as a source of unpaid labour or targeting a woman to rape. Once you see a person as an object, you are able to treat that person like an object because he or she has ceased to exist in your imagination as a real live human being and instead is reduced to the status of a thing. You can then mentally and physically manoeuvre this 'object' to serve your own ends. Once you deny this object any full-bodied existence and attach a label – for example, Paki, enemy, terrorist, whore, queer or scum – you can stay safe in denial of any cruelty or pain you inflict on another human being.

Having an object in mind also serves another function: mentally, we confer a higher status, attributing them with qualities we don't possess ourselves. We can then look up to and adore these objects, envy and attack them, defend or control them. Or we reverse the position and imagine an object as a representation of those aspects of ourselves that we don't like or reject because we feel ashamed of them. Then we can look down on this object/person and despise it, punish it, knock it about a bit or even try to bring it up to our own superior level.

This psychological process is evidenced on a social and national scale. Throughout the aggression of history witches, prostitutes, homosexuals, Catholics, lepers have been among those demonised into objects which represented (and can still represent) various kinds of evil, temptation, or danger from lower or baser aspects of oneself. These aspects threaten to overwhelm the acceptable parts of the self and cannot be tolerated; rejection, exclusion or sometimes terrible acts of violence become the sole means of alleviating our sense of threat.

The dimension of sexism adds its own special conviction: negativity (fear, mistrust and revilement) of the female body. Once a man thinks of and sees a woman's body as an object, he feels he has a right to treat 'it' as he wants. 'It' becomes his 'property' to penetrate, slap around, intimidate or bully. When the chips are down, when men are made redundant, when the poor are poor, in the middle of war, men will often vent their frustrations on objects 'lower' than themselves: first in line are women's bodies, followed by children. Powerlessness is briefly assuaged by domination over *something*.

Violence may be associated with hatred but even men who love and adore their women can treat them as objects – whether a woman's body is the object of desire, revilement, lust, adornment or the butt on which a man takes out every frustration in his life, her body is still his property.

The mental association of female bodies with object status is revealed in biased attitudes as well: women can be victims of violence in many ways which leave no visible scars or bruises. A social worker is reluctant to commit a father he knows is sexually abusing his daughter because the girl doesn't seem too traumatised by what has happened. A policeman is slow to take action when a wife is beaten by her husband; he sympathises with the man because she wants a divorce. A well-known columnist viciously attacks a female TV presenter for being too old and too ugly to appear on the screen: there is no public clamour for an apology because he is judged to be voicing a self-evident truth. A clever lawyer persists in getting a rape victim to recall every detail of an abusive attack because he can prove she has a vivid imagination and use it to weaken her testimony. A judge grants a rapist a lenient sentence because he gathers the victim led a 'promiscuous' lifestyle. A priest reproaches a woman for considering contraception because he doesn't see the already over-stressed and exhausted human being in front of him, only a female body whose reproductive capacity is the sole legitimacy of her existence. A widow of a man who has died from HIV/AIDS in East Africa finds herself accused of bringing illness into the family: her land is confiscated and she is forced to live with her children on the margins of society. A consultant surgeon allows a woman patient in his care to be examined vaginally by medical students while she is anaesthetised for unrelated surgery because he cannot see the harm in it; after all, it's a good learning opportunity for his students.

What binds these examples together is the fact that the way men think about women's bodies – consciously and unconsciously – affects their *treatment* of women. Once you begin to connect the dots, you find a fairly coherent picture emerging. None of these examples indicates individual pathology but together they illustrate the consequences of being brought up in any culture which teaches men that women's bodies are inferior objects.

There is a further problem. If this were the end of the story, we might have witnessed a far more widespread and effective challenge; far more protest from women individually and collectively about being treated in this manner. The lack of significant protest actually helps to explain why the whole issue of objectification of women's bodies is not trivial, why it cannot be reduced to a question of showing disrespect by exhibiting calendars of naked women on the office wall.

There is so much more at stake. If men are to understand what feminism is opposing, it is crucial to recognise that the harm done to women's bodies has a pernicious and less visible effect on women's attitudes to their own bodies. This is why the next chapter looks in more detail at the effects of sexism on the female psyche.

7
SEXISM AND THE FEMALE PSYCHE

The kernel of sexism, remember, is the inferiority of a woman's body. It's not that every parent wants a son or that little girls are unloved: the point is that being in a female body has very different implications for self-esteem within a sexual, social, professional and emotional context. As a corollary of a woman's genitals being so reviled, the rest of her body also assumes a generalised negativity by association, like an apple which is essentially and unavoidably infected by some unseen rot at its core.

As a consequence, it is rare to meet a woman who is happy with her body *as it is*, who is comfortable and celebratory of her body not just when she has reached an ideal weight or fits into a favourite pair of jeans but who actually loves her body as it is naturally, with all its fluctuations and changes and natural rhythms. Men often express some dissatisfaction with their bodies and may wish to be fitter or develop specific muscles to demonstrate their masculinity, but my observation is that few men are afflicted with such a profound sense of critical alienation from their bodies.

When a woman's body is defined as incomplete and powerless, female aspects of the body become downgraded to faults that many women try to eliminate. This ranges from hiding menstruation, to morbid obsession with eradicating smell – perfumed tampons during our periods, perfumed mini-pads in between, perfumed douches just in case – to removing evidence of what doesn't conform to the internalised ideal (Western) model. State-of-the-art features include flawless, smooth, young skin; tight-ass; firm breasts, long-legs, narrow waist; billowing hair; pouty lips and come-hither eyes. No place here for cellulite, hair on any part of the skin (other than the head), smell, flab, roll or wrinkle.

Unsurprisingly, women of all ages and all classes and all nationalities – the vast majority of women – find fault with their bodies. Women do not like their bodies as they are *naturally*.

If we could count up the hours, days, months spent in contemplation of appearance, the critiquing of different body parts and all the efforts at concealment, eradication, disguise, removal, enhancement or reduction, we would find a colossal amount of energy consumed as well as a colossal amount of money spent on purchase of products, treatments and services.

It is my experience that one of the hardest tasks for any woman in this world is to reclaim her body, seen for so long as an object, and transform it into a dimension of herself that she cherishes, inside and out. This is because the pressure of continuous awareness of her body as an object in others' eyes has taught her to see it as an object in her own eyes too.

Early in life, a girl's body ceases to belong to her. She becomes aware of the cultural emphasis on being attractive and the need to present herself in a certain manner. She learns the importance of external image: how she looks becomes more significant than who she is inside. This sows the seed of a burgeoning and lifelong self-consciousness. From this moment, she will begin to compare and compete with other girls for the right to be considered an attractive object. The unity and integrity of body, mind and spirit is at this point broken. Her physical identity and self-hood are split: who she is versus how she needs to be seen. Living this divide usually lasts for life.

Whether she puts all her efforts into endorsing the feminine function or rebelling against it, this process affects every young girl. Some become tomboys; some develop anorexia to try and put off developing physically into womanhood. Many put their efforts from an early age into being as feminine and as attractive as possible. The catch is that those women who are adored for their bodies as they naturally occur are a fortunate minority. For most women, having a female body entails a lifelong struggle to suppress the natural in favour of an imposed and artificial ideal.

Current trends to 'sexualise' little girls before puberty, turning them into self-conscious objects at an increasingly younger age, mean that even those few precious years of bodily integrity – when there is no division between mind and body – are ever dwindling. Self-consciousness starts earlier and, with the aid of medication or surgery, the struggle with nature now lasts longer.

The pre-occupation with making good an inherent flaw has been around for a very long time. So, in some ways, we take this effort for granted. Fashions change; women's feet are no longer bound or female waists squeezed into breath-constricting corsets. Modern women feel liberated from such restraints and yet, at the same time, we remain unconcerned about the hugely increasing 'normality' of cosmetic surgery often undertaken as lightly as altering the curtains or replacing the fridge.

If you have the money, you can 'defeat' nature, whether you're sixteen in South America wanting a boob job to increase your chances of marriage, thirty-six in North America, seeking a designer vagina to boost your sex ratings or fifty-six in Europe, eager to remove bodily indications of ageing. You don't need encouragement or coercion from an individual partner. Once you've internalised your object status so well and for so long, you can believe that there is really no harm in it, it's just fun – and who doesn't want to look good?

The mechanics of surgery – cutting, slicing, bruising and breaking – are transformed into elegant euphemisms of lifting, augmenting, shaping and re-aligning. We seem to forget that unlike applying make-up or colouring hair, cosmetic surgery cannot be reversed or taken away; that procedures often have to be repeated after a time to maintain the desired effect.

Many women insist that this is all part of women's right to choose. Surgical intervention is promoted as an aspect of liberation because breast enlargement, facelifts, liposuction and buttock reduction or implants mean you now don't have to be lumbered with a natural woman's body. Today, in our own culture, there is access to vaccinations which suppress our periods for five or even ten years or to caesarian surgery as an option to avoid the pain of natural birth: anything, *anything* is better than having to put up with the hassle, inconvenience and nuisance of being born into a female body.

Self-Image

I believe the repercussions of seeing one's body as an object spread even further. Alienation from one's physical being soon encompasses one's psychological being. Girls learn very early on in life that 'attractive' behaviour goes hand in hand with attractive appearance. Be pleasing, smiling and sympathetic; avoid anger, disagreement, unkindness, rudeness or wilfulness. This dual psycho-physical imperative of pleasing others becomes for the majority of women a lifetime's preoccupation.

I have spent over three decades working with thousands of women – from many different backgrounds – and I've witnessed first-hand the repercussions of this imperative. Despite cultural variations, common denominators repeatedly emerge: difficulty in stating what they want; inability to say 'no' or to express anger. Always at the core is low self-esteem linked to poor body image.

Related psychological symptoms are lack of confidence and uncertainty. This may be experienced as a fear of speaking up in public or of using one's voice; the inability to interrupt someone or to express an opinion which differs from the majority or problems with challenging others' behaviour. Women have an extraordinary capacity to undermine themselves with anxiety about how they're seen, which erodes their ability to be authoritative when they need to be: alongside undoubted external competence, women often torture themselves with internal self-criticism and a sense of inadequacy. An inordinate dependence on others' approval becomes a major obstacle to emotional and physical autonomy.

Individual women's mental health or mental illness cannot be separated from the much broader experience of socialisation. Women wouldn't be nearly so affected, wound up or demolished by the behaviour and attitudes of others were it not for the existence of a latent conviction that, for some reason, they don't deserve better. It isn't logical. It isn't rational. But it is there. Individual self-image is an intrinsic part of an entire psychological syndrome constructed around an internal and invisible belief system that is an inevitable consequence of seeing their position always and forever on a *lower* rung.

The vast majority of interpersonal problems in women arise from internal fault-finding stemming from perceptions based in this belief system. The experience of teaching and working with women for so many years has been a major catalyst in my own evolving consciousness-raising process. What has made me into a committed feminist is my own observation of how chronic anxiety and hyper-critical self-image lead to consistently repeated patterns of behaviour: alternation between keeping quiet and swallowing everything and then suddenly lashing out in frustration, often viciously; the propensity for self-blame even when victims of others' aggression; and a pervasive sense of powerless born of a lack of permission to fully express oneself.

These women I have worked with closely over the years cannot be dismissed as wimps or shrinking violets: these are often capable, achieving, strong women. Not just English or reserved; they belong to no particular age group or class or income bracket or nationality; no physical type, no educational type; no particular creed or colour of skin; no particular psychological or physical profile. These are not women who are all introverts or neurotic. So either one concludes that these thousands of women happen coincidentally to be personally pathetic or one looks for a common denominator: the only one I have found is that they are women in this world.

8
A MUTED CULTURE

From physical inequality to spiritual inequality to social inequality, does the influence of sexism stop there? Unfortunately no. There are many other aspects of life which seem remote from the issue of gender but which are still affected by inequality: another subtle but visible outcome is that qualities associated with the male gender have become established as preferable (dominant) while other qualities have acquired a backseat status (muted).

By following the threads we uncover a distinct pattern: elaborately woven over time to the present day, we find that nearly everything associated with the female body or female aptitudes has ended up being assigned an 'inferior' status. Take the innocuous example of attitudes to domestic labour. The human biological imperative determines that both genders are necessary for reproduction to occur so one might assume that the role is split but equal. How then did it transpire that our male ancestors convinced themselves that the tasks they carried out like hunting, fishing and fighting were far more valuable and significant than domestic tasks and child-rearing? Three millennia later the repercussions were still in evidence when feminists first began to fight to be able to get out of the home into paid work and then to be paid equally within the workplace. The underlying assumption all along is that only paid employment – real work – is valued.

This hasn't changed today. It is no coincidence that we have come to value the sphere of men's work and achievements – traditionally outside the home like bringing in food and supplies and eventually money – much more than the maintenance of the home, housework, cooking and child care when one could have logically concluded that both roles were equally (but differently) vital to the welfare, growth and nurture of the future generation.

Real work has been rewarded monetarily because it is valued while women have traditionally laboured for nothing. Mother's Day (a modern version following the ancient custom of Mothering Sunday) is taken to represent adequate compensation for the other three hundred and sixty-four days taken up with mothering responsibilities and chores. Moreover, many young women today express little or no interest in housework, cooking, sewing and in some instances even child care because they find these activities intrinsically unrewarding. Gadgets of all kinds and prepared foods save a modern woman from having to do menial and insignificant tasks since career recognition and achievement in the workplace have far more kudos and importance.

Finding domestic tasks menial, though, doesn't mean that women don't do them any more. Recent cross-national research shows that women still do the lion's share of domestic chores in a household where both partners are in full-time employment. Many of today's working mothers, in turn, would not be able to manage without a global care chain which supplies poorer women from less developed parts of the world to look after richer women's children so that they themselves can pay for the education of their own children who have to be looked after by (female) family members back home.

Once you begin to see a few threads, you find them everywhere. Psychological qualities associated with male and female stereotypes have also become graded – valued more or less – rather than equal. The realm of emotion, for example, is messy, unpredictable, childish (associated with the female of the human species). It is regarded as inferior to the faculty of reason (in which men apparently excel) which is therefore celebrated as cool, cerebral, clear, analytical, logical, linear, 'evidence-based' and above all *superior*. Making sense matters if you want to be taken seriously. Science has become a sacred cow making evidence-based knowledge the sole defining factor in what is valid and invalid in life while wisdom and (female) intuition have been relegated to cloud-cuckoo land: cute but ultimately irrelevant.

These issues may appear trivial in themselves but, taken as part of the whole, they are far from insignificant. Irrevocably etched in our minds and hearts are assumptions that some ways of being, thinking and behaving are more important than others; that some ways of seeing the world are more valid and significant while, correspondingly, alternatives ways (intuitive, emotional, cyclical) are dismissed or trivialised. We are taught and encouraged in some modes of being and learn that other modes are fanciful or abnormal. We end up with a complex dualistic system where every aspect of life can be subjected to a higher and a lower weighting.

Instead of seeing two different qualities or characteristics as *complementary* – as with yin and yang – we assume them not only to be opposite but, more importantly, one evolves into an accepted norm while the other becomes marginalised. The emphasis on one or other aspect affects personal and social choices of every kind. Do you accommodate immigrants or exclude them? Do children benefit more from competition or cooperation? Should a boss be financially rewarded even though this means his employees lose out? Is external image that much more important than internal quantities?

Hierarchy	v.	Equality
Individual	v.	Community
Reason	v.	Emotion
Self	v.	Other
Doing	v.	Being
Division	v.	Connection
Exclusion	v.	Accommodation
Self as separate	v.	Self as part of the whole
Linear	v.	Cyclical
Competition	v.	Collaboration
Unit	v.	Context
Outer	v.	Inner

These lists do not immediately equate with male/masculine versus female/feminine The reality of human experience –

a mixture of nature and nurture – is too complex to be able to make such an easy conclusion. As humans, we can often identify a personally familiar mode of being. Many of us gravitate towards one group more than the other while some people move easily between the two modes. Some individuals who resonate more with the muted aspects often find they have to adapt to succeed or fit into the dominant culture.

These could all be complementary aspects of life but they're not seen like that. The process of ageing, for example, is officially conceived as a single chronological line of physical and mental decline from birth to death. Another way of viewing the passage of life is to see stages, phases and cycles of transition: this doesn't negate the timeline but it offers more accurately and more fully what an individual actually experiences. Both perceptions contribute to the whole but in commercial, medical, economic and social spheres, the linear perception runs the show exclusively.

Why is a dominant cultural preference for one way of seeing the world relevant to sexism? One immediate consequence is that the tendency to compartmentalise – unit over context – skews our perceptions. This particular lens enables us to treat others as objects, even if coercion is not applied. It enables us to opt for sexual gratification without strings, finding someone to fuck without emotional entanglement. Another consequence is that an exclusive focus on unit and division blocks from view all the connecting links between what we categorise as unacceptable and acceptable manifestations of sexism.

Through the lens of division we disconnect the acceptable from the unacceptable: we interpret extreme acts of sexism as isolated incidents rather than acknowledging an entire web of interconnecting threads. Seeing through the lens of connection makes it possible to consider the disturbing reality that those unacceptable outcomes originate and flourish in an entire context of sexism – commonplace thoughts, words, biases and assumptions, some of which barely register in our awareness.

9
RAPE BEGINS AT HOME

This is a provocative proposition, but what follows is a necessary challenge to one of the pivotal mainstays of sexism: the apparent reluctance to address the incidence of rape through a failure to comprehend the true violation of forced penetration. I heard the phrase first used by a man interviewed on the radio earlier this year during a programme reporting on the high incidence of rape and sexual abuse of children in South Africa (according to national statistics, one man in four admits to raping a woman at some time in his life). The focus on South Africa was prompted directly in response to an especially gruesome and violent rape of a young girl in that country who died from her appalling injuries. Some of the people being interviewed felt that this could be their 'Delhi moment', a reference to the public outpouring of anger after the gang rape of a young Indian medical student on a bus at the end of last year who also died from her horrific injuries.

Of course these are instances of extreme sexual violence but as long as rape remains at the far end of the spectrum and conveniently disconnected from the rest of sexist behaviour, it remains possible for all the minor and unremarkable acts of psychological violence – in our homes, our schools, our universities, our places of employment, our courts and on our streets – to go unchallenged if not unnoticed.

If we look at sexism as an interconnecting web of patriarchal beliefs – physical, mental, social and cultural – we uncover uncomfortable implications. We begin with the absolute 'given' that the female body is less valuable than the male body; less valuable socially, monetarily, spiritually and aesthetically. Once established as inferior to the male, and in our present system with whatever particular cultural variations, male power over the female body (subject status over object status) will be at the centre of a whole range of restrictions at every level of life.

Those born male will first witness this and learn to do the same, through direct instruction and modelling or indirect absorption of cultural norms. Growing male children will learn to assume some kind of superiority – without anything having to be said out loud – and as they grow up and develop sexually they will also learn from their own background how to treat females, find partners, establish families and continue their own lineage. In Western cultures, we can add the likely exposure to a generous dose of media bias, lads' magazines and easily accessible pornographic 'lessons' in mechanical sexual encounters which portray as much humanity as an instruction manual in engineering. As a consequence it is difficult to see how any young male can avoid exposure to the assumption of *permission* to regard a female as lower than himself or to treat her body as an object, even though personal, cultural, and social factors will determine individual outcomes.

Most people would agree that rape is bad and should not happen: in principle it is generally unacceptable. The problem is that rape as a crime is seen as an isolated unit of behaviour, not a symptom of sexism embedded in the entire context of sexist upbringing – hence the title of this chapter. We tend not to see the connections between the specific act of rape and small (apparently insignificant) remarks, thoughts, gestures, assumptions which are a conditioned response to the gender of the human being in front of us. Sexism is so deeply imprinted on our psyches that we discount the existence of any links between the general and the particular. Refusal to see any connection allows continuing anti-female bias to flourish.

This explains why it is still not at all uncommon today for women of all ages to encounter hostility when they are victims of rape: from educational institutions if they report a rape while they are students or within legal institutions when they give evidence. Rape victims face stonewalling from state institutions, like the tens of thousands of Muslim women, systematically raped during the Bosnian war, who have still received nothing in the way of recognition or support that they were promised over eighteen years ago and have been fighting for ever since. Rape victims can themselves be transformed into villains as happened recently in the US when a gang of rapists (identified through social media evidence taken at the scene of the attack) happened to include members of a hallowed football team. The young woman faced widespread condemnation within her local community for speaking out because she was judged to have scuppered their promising sporting careers.

For me, this last example highlights a curious blind spot in many men's cognitive functioning. I am willing to concede that men are passionate about sport; that football is hugely important to the Americans and even that talented young men should be encouraged in their future careers. However, I would like to ask men if they, in turn, could consider for once the actual *experience*, the physical and psychological impact, of being raped. This part of the story is conveniently overlooked.

The tendency to downplay rape is not logically defensible but then this isn't about logic. When it comes to kneejerk responses, sexist conditioning blots out reason and all that 'hard scientific evidence' so favoured by the dominant culture. The deep-down conviction that women invite, fantasise about or even secretly enjoy rape continues to exert an inordinate power individually and collectively over the male psyche despite the facts.

So what are these facts? With sexual contact of any kind, the physical experience of *pleasure* depends entirely on arousal of the genital tissue which becomes engorged with blood. When a woman is raped, the process of sexual arousal never gets going: fear shuts down all the relevant neuro-physiological systems and, as a direct consequence, blood flow decreases in her genital area. Her vagina may be opened and forced penetration is possible but as the nerve endings in the skin do not have the benefit of the effects of arousal, her vagina remains tight and taut. The physical experience of forced entry by an erect penis is one of extreme pain with frequent laceration of the vaginal wall and severe internal bruising.

RAPE BEGINS AT HOME

All medical examiners of rape victims in any part of the world will attest to this and yet the 'dumbing down' of the crime of rape of women stands as a true testament to the power of patriarchal thinking: never mind the facts, we believe what we want to believe. That murky unconscious legacy about women's bodies – object/cunt/evil/dangerous – exercises far more influence over our minds and attitudes than any scientific data.

Although young boys are abused and some men are occasionally raped, it is overwhelmingly women and girls who are victims of rape. We hesitate to admit this. The programme I mentioned earlier also featured a local radio station's imaginative and effective device for rousing their listeners from complacent indifference. Throughout one entire day, a buzzer was sounded every four minutes to alert the audience to the fact that a rape was occurring every four minutes in their country. Each time, the broadcaster announced, 'Every four minutes someone is raping somebody here in South Africa.' *Someone. Somebody.* Why is it so hard for us to acknowledge that it is *men* who are raping *women*?

Rape is never a question of sexual activity: it is a question of power. Children are abused by adults because adults have power (at many levels) over children. Women are raped because men have power over them. The truth of this kind of statement appears to be difficult to stomach. Defensive protests – from both men and women – are quick to emerge: but men get raped too; men are abused as children too; men are victims of domestic violence as well; women have more power in the home; my boss is a woman and she is much worse than any man.

Similarly, try pointing to evidence that depressive patients are more than twice as likely to be women; those on medication for anxiety are ten times more likely to be women; sixty per cent of anorexia sufferers are female ranging from pubescent girls to middle-aged women; domestic violence towards women is a global phenomenon. You can guarantee that protest will quickly follow: men get depressed too; I know a man on tranquillisers; women hit men sometimes; men are just as concerned about their appearance these days.

Denial is a familiar feature of contemporary responses to sexism. At the time of writing there has been much made of sixteen-year-old Malala Yousafzai's address to the UN on the issue of 'children's' education. The facts have again been fudged: the reason she was almost killed by being deliberately shot in the head last year was not because she was a child but because she was *female*. Although she spoke in her address about her personal focus on women's rights and girls' education, any allusion to sexism (i.e. inequality between girls and boys) in reports by the general media has been conveniently airbrushed out of the picture.

When news spread through social media recently, exposing images of a well-known TV presenter being abused at the hands of her husband, millions of words were written about domestic abuse but there was no mention of sexism. Somehow we are persuaded that this wealthy, well-regarded individual – 'a pillar of society' – had simply exhibited some aberrant behaviour (for which he received the tellingly severe punishment of a police caution). Nobody openly places domestic abuse in the context of sexism because, as a civilised society, we're supposed to have finished with all that now. As long as we continue to deny the interconnection between the sexist persuasion – a woman's body as object – and acts of sexual harassment, sexual assault, domestic violence and rape, nothing will change.

10
A CORE AMBIVALENCE

Does it matter if nothing changes? Isn't rape just one facet of a regrettably violent world that we have to learn to live with? When you think of so much slaughter of innocent people through terrorist or counter-terrorist activity, why should the rape of a few women require special attention? The answer lies in the psychological repercussions on women who witness the social response to rape. I have already described the phenomenon of a poor body image on a woman's mental health. As long as sexual violence goes unpunished or treated lightly, as long as women are somehow held responsible, all young girls and adult women will be reminded that their bodies are worth nothing. It reconfirms again and again women's status as objects.

It is essentially a question of value. An object is not a whole person to be valued. I have never met or worked with a woman who had been raped or battered who actually wanted to castrate the man involved. More than anything these women want the perpetrators to see the harm they've done: to see, really see the pain caused, the profound damage, the trauma and theft of something irreplaceable; to understand rape as a physical and psychological *violation*. Acknowledging the hurt and suffering they have perpetrated and feeling some genuine remorse could initiate in men a shift of consciousness.

In the early sessions of a programme designed to help men who had been convicted of domestic violence towards their female partners, I would put up a large blank piece of paper on the wall and, gradually, each man in the group would be invited – overcoming understandable reluctance – to describe the injuries they had inflicted on women. Eventually each item and each occurrence added up to a very long list; looking at them together in an uncomfortable silence was an extremely confronting experience. It was the first time these men had begun to genuinely take account of their behaviour. From 'something just comes over me' or 'I can't help it' to the dawning of responsibility. This was not an exercise to induce guilt but an opportunity to come face to face with the unavoidable reality that the object they used to act out their aggression was actually a human being. Acknowledgment of violation is what can begin to heal, not apologies or chocolates and flowers.

Recognition is a necessary start to transforming such behaviour. Rape survivors are unlikely ever to receive such recognition. There are dramatic and arresting adverts to strike home the impact of drink driving on human lives but where is there a campaign to show men the deep and often permanent damage they cause when they abuse or rape women?

As I write this, I am thinking about the parents of Trayvor Martin, the young African American boy shot and killed by George Zimmerman who was subsequently found not guilty of either murder or manslaughter. The response has been one of shock and rage and many have spoken about the appalling message it sends to young black boys: that they have no value in society. I agree with this entirely but it also makes me wonder why we don't ever witness as much protest about women being raped.

It is impossible to avoid comparing the typical media response to the rape of a male – shock, horror, outrage – in contrast to the response to the rape of a woman. Unless she is murdered, a raped woman doesn't make the headlines. The reality is that rape of a woman is regarded as unfortunate, yes, but fairly ordinary, almost inevitable, rather like the traditional approach to boys and masturbation: regrettable but what can you do about it? Boys will be boys.

Some men are brutally and sexually abused as small boys. This should never happen but the press does not report this as ordinary everyday phenomena. It is not the norm. Those acts occur when the system breaks down: we understand this as extreme behaviour and no mercy is shown to the perpetrators. Unlike rape of women, there is no ambivalence about the horror (and unacceptability) of such crimes.

It doesn't help that many men's unthinking sexist habits are coloured by their personal fantasies: lusting after the young 'tart' in the office or about how they would like their wives to behave in bed. This is not something they would willingly admit to so they tend to put them to one side, yet the power of these fantasies – whether or not they are acted out – functions as a deterrent to collective responsibility.

Another major deterrent is the pervasive influence of myths about male sexuality which continue to exert psychological power in social consciousness. Man's urgent and overriding need for sex, for example, has evolved into an unspoken but implicit mitigating factor where personal and social attitudes to rape are concerned. This is one clear example of where the biological imperative has been conveniently hijacked by patriarchal brainwashing. Men have high sex drives – especially when younger – but as many men know perfectly well, even when a man is hot and horny, he is still capable of enough respect for his female partner not to override any sign of her reluctance. He can choose to honour a boundary, even when he would much prefer not to. It is only when sexist distortion – permission to exert power over woman's body as object – enters the picture that the capacity for choice conveniently disappears. Dumbing down the violation of rape will continue as long as men are believed to have uncontrollable sexual needs and women's bodies are regarded as vehicles of release.

Even if a girl grows up with a father who cherishes her, a mother who teaches her about women's strength and brothers who love and respect her, she will still learn from the culture to be afraid. Researchers of the widespread phenomenon called 'the safety gap' contrast men's and women's experience of feeling safe on the streets, in public places, when travelling, in the workplace and even in their own homes. The more developed the country, the wider the gap.

It is impossible for women to remain unaffected by stories of violence towards females on the news and in the press every week and many commentators have denounced the increase of detailed depictions of torture, rape, mutilation and murder of women in television dramas and feature films. None of this is coincidental. None of this is unconnected.

It is hardly surprising that many women give themselves up to sexual pleasure with a man feeling extremely grateful for their good fortune. A man they can trust, they hope, despite so many unanswered questions: why do men rape women? Why do men predate on children? Why do men batter women? Why do they use words that revile women's anatomy? The focus on the importance of depth of penetration into the vagina eclipses what also matters: a yearning for emotional penetration into hearts and minds. Women sometimes long to be seen, to be known, not as objects, but multi-dimensionally.

It's unlikely that women themselves will ever form a protest march against the incidence of rape. If ever those who had been raped courageously 'came out' and formed such a march, it would be surprising to see the sheer numbers. It might show once and for all that *all* women – not just the young tarty ones who 'ask for it' – are at risk of being raped; old, young and middle-aged alike. How many mothers or fathers protest when their daughters are raped?

To understand why women don't protest publically (or even privately a lot of the time), we have to go back to the issue of body as object: women's bodies are transformed into objects in their *own* personal perception. Despite all efforts to be pleasing and attractive, female bodies are ultimately a source of disappointment because they will not conform. Every aspect of the female body defines it as non-linear. Women bleed. Women's bodies are round and soft and fleshy. They are unpredictable, curved, messy, chaotic and susceptible to rhythmic changes. Women frequently experience emotions that can't be explained logically. One of the reasons women feel so often alienated from their bodies is because they have come to regard them as objects of betrayal.

Sexism is especially pernicious in its effect because it is based on an aspect of women that cannot be altered. However much women aspire to equality and however much they strive to get it right, the bottom line is that, apart from trans-gender exceptions, the female body at birth remains a female body for life.

This leads to an emotional ambivalence. On one side, a woman's body is an essential part of her value to men. Her body is seen as a safe haven, a source of comfort, release, decoration and pleasure. It is a vital vehicle and carrier of reproduction. Her body can offer a refuge from an unemotional, linear world.

On the other side, it is this very flesh, this interior space and female genitalia that defines her position. A woman's body is *at the same time* the cause of her 'lower position' in the patriarchal system (i.e. she's not a man) and potentially her best asset in terms of status and survival within it. From this paradox arises an ambivalence and uncertainty which lie at the heart of women's powerlessness.

Once you comprehend this ambivalence, you start to understand why so many women – even after being raped –

take so long, if ever, to feel rage and more often get trapped in self-blame and depression. You begin to see what makes a strong independent woman respond with extreme docility when she is physically assaulted by a lover; why women persist in returning to abusive partners; why women don't protest collectively about continuing to live in fear of violence. You begin to understand why women continue to uphold a system which is based on an absolute *lie*, as if female inferiority really were an unquestionable truth.

I believe it also sheds light on another central anomaly. Despite all the achievements of feminist struggles in the past and despite efforts at many levels to encourage women to be more self-affirming – despite so many extraordinary advances in human development, scientific understanding, creative enterprise and invention leading to a rejection of so many historical myths that held sway in the past – genuine equality continues to elude us. At many levels, humankind is still held in thrall to the bogus assumption of female inferiority.

11
YOU DON'T NEED TO BE VEILED TO BE VOICELESS

I set out in this book to encourage men to espouse the feminist cause because there is much more at stake than fighting for equal pay and equal opportunities. I have tried to illustrate the psychological repercussions for women of living within a patriarchal culture that regards the female body as inferior and relegates it to object status. I have also proposed that the seeds of violent behaviour towards women are sown and grown within this particular culture.

I imagine that many men will find this hard to fathom. How does one reconcile the received opinion that women are so much more liberated and equal than their grandmothers, with what I am suggesting is a common experience of low physical and psychological self-esteem? Most women appear to be fine so perhaps I'm exaggerating or over-stating my case? Isn't what I am talking about only relevant to cultures where women are kept hidden and out of the public eye or at least very obviously disadvantaged?

I sympathise with this puzzlement to some extent because women tend to hide self-doubt. Women become adept at keeping the show on the road, coping, functioning and presenting an outside image of confidence and capability. We excel at impression management and hiding vulnerability.

The workplace makes an interesting illustration of this disparity because it is, in itself, a microcosm of sexist culture. On the surface, visible improvements have been made with more women in higher positions but despite external confidence, anxiety often persists on the inside. Many women – in many parts of the world and at every level of the professional hierarchy – describe their experience of problems of communication and handling authority; their reluctance to criticise or challenge subordinates, colleagues or bosses; their feeling deeply conflicted about family and professional demands while observing that they work much harder than their male counterparts. Below are the kinds of recurring problems admitted to by women when they can let their guard down and feel safe to acknowledge the truth:

- 'I find myself intimidated when speaking to my male boss'
- 'I find it impossible to deal with male aggression'
- 'It is hard for me to interrupt someone in public'
- 'I don't really belong because I'm excluded from the after-hours social networking'
- 'I keep quiet even when I know I'm being putdown'
- 'It isn't easy to be angry because I don't want to appear unpleasant'
- 'It's hard for me to refuse because I don't want to appear unfriendly'
- 'I don't know how to challenge unfair criticism'
- 'I can't challenge negative remarks about my body (because secretly I think they're right)'
- 'You know your appearance is scrutinised when you come into work'

- 'I don't express my anger because I'd let too much come out'
- 'I find it difficult to handle authority because I'm not sure I have an equal right to be here'
- 'How do I challenge a male manager who is incompetent but likely to get nasty?'
- 'Sometimes I don't know if I can really take my perceptions seriously'
- 'I find it hard to challenge the status quo and bring in something new'

Regular (usually politically motivated) initiatives to get more women into this or that domain concentrate on raising numbers rather than looking at the internal experience, which is why they tend to fail. If the quality of the working experience was the focus rather than boosting statistical ratios, it might be better understood that the starting place for women is different from that of men. A different starting place means 'equality of opportunity' ends up being a meaningless phrase, largely due to the process of emulation.

Emulation Not Innovation

Remember the dynamic between the muted and the dominant group: when a muted group moves upwards, it tends to become absorbed into the culture of the dominant group. To identify with the dominant group the lower group adopts some or all of what it sees as 'superior' features.

This can include physical features. If you look at presenters on Japanese television today, for instance, at photos of call girls advertising their wares or young women in commercials, you notice an overwhelming preponderance of Japanese girls with 'non-Japanese' eyes. Some have naturally wider eyes – like Westerners – while others submit to surgery to get their eyes widened to boost their careers. It is obvious which is prized more highly in terms of being successful. Similarly many women on the African continent spend a lot of time and money on skin-whitening products despite the harm these substances can do to their skin. Why? Because the paler the skin, the more attractive it is deemed to be. The motivation for women to eliminate roundness, softness and curves from their bodies in favour of taut, tight, firm, strong muscular flesh is part of a similar process of emulation: the psychological equivalent is deriding weakness, vulnerability, failure, slowness and emotionality because they're not associated with masculinity.

The tendency towards emulation leads women into a bit of a trap. The goal of feminism has always been to win for women the same rights and power as men: this includes material gains, increased status and improved access to educational and professional opportunities. Equality has also come to imply the right to the same privileges. Women go to male strip shows because men have been enjoying such entertainment for centuries. The 'laddettes' emulate predatory ways and scrutinise prospective male partners ('gorgeous bum', 'huge box', 'great pecks') as potential objects of sexual conquest. If men can have sex without strings, then women can do likewise.

When Freud described penis envy as a symptom of women's psychopathology, he was describing one tangible fragment, not the whole picture. Few women actually want to be a man or envy a man his penis but I believe the majority of women have occasion to envy the privilege that goes with it: whoever is higher up is envied because they have more power. In an effort to fit in, women copy and adopt the same goals in an effort to make the system their own. It was once about wearing trousers, smoking, swearing, driving, flying and daring exploits; now it's about being the boss and having it all.

When women enter the game as players themselves, they learn to adapt to the rules of that game. Many women are required to display those characteristics associated with having balls if they are to be accepted, supported and respected on equal terms with the real guys. To achieve 'equal' status and respect – not just a title – in the workplace, for example, a woman cannot continue to behave like a woman is 'supposed' to behave. If you're not sure what that implies, try emotional, caring and attentive towards others; indecisive, sensitive to criticism, susceptible; a tendency to be indirect, imprecise and a lack of staying power when the going gets tough.

Emulating the male way means conforming to a certain style of behaviour: generally determined, unwavering and unemotional. Preferred behaviour includes being focused, competitive, tough, ruthless, self-interested and capable of putting others' needs and feelings right out of the picture when it interferes with the main target, usually of increasing profit. Some women feel completely at home in this environment; many others do not but need to conform to stay in their jobs so are unlikely to use their positions to challenge the norm, remaining passively instrumental in its maintenance.

The overall outcome is that although the position of some of the players has changed, the game remains the same. Somewhere along the line, patriarchal invention and meaning has taken over and the course of feminism has been determined by a single frame of reference: women tend to reflect back the same unquestioned values about what is and what isn't important in life. Even when it begins to feel equal, it only takes one remark, one incident, one putdown, one rejection…to bring women face to face with the fact (and there is often genuine surprise) that this means being equal in a *man's* world.

Of course women do not take everything lying down. We get angry, usually expressed as aggression – sometimes out loud, sometimes indirectly – at home, at work, on the road, everywhere. We can get nasty too; we avoid speaking the truth because men 'can't take it' or belittle whatever efforts men do make, confiding to other women 'how pathetic they all are', taking an inverse satisfaction in being the real superiors.

When girls today form the same gangs as the boys and spit on the old and frail, the young and pathetic, it alleviates the feeling of having no power but only for a short while.

Despite all the strategies for survival, powerlessness persists because the principles of patriarchy to which women subscribe are inherently and forever *incapable* of seeing both genders as equal.

Occasionally resentment becomes collectively focused and organised into political or anarchical activity: lobbying, demonstrations, feminist manifestos and radicalism. Hostility to men and a wish to turn the tables (reverse the positions of the ladder) can add momentum and it is difficult to keep aggression and revenge completely out of the picture. This means that many women are afraid of their own anger because all they see is the possibility of aggression. The fantasy of an inversion of the dominant order (women *over* men) is terrifying: what would we do without men? We need them and we love them.

Women's love for the men in their lives is in large part what binds them to sexism. They love men dearly but also depend on them. Meeting others' needs is evidence of self-worth but when loving and pleasing others become blurred, devotion is less the outcome of a generous (and equal) heart and more a measure of dependence on others' approval. Dependence increases the fear of losing the love of men. Where would we be without it? *Who* would we be without it? The unimaginable keeps too many women trapped in self-perpetuating cycles of frustration and self-doubt.

12
THE UNAVOIDABLE ISSUE
OF POWER

A byproduct of seeing feminism as a women's thing is that men can feel excluded, uncertain and often resentful. I remember twenty years ago when women's newly emerging sexual assertiveness was openly held responsible for the increased incidence of male erectile dysfunction. Fortunately, the pharmaceutical industry came up with Viagra so we could all breathe a sigh of relief again.

Part of the response to gender uncertainty has generated movements like Iron John or the Kingdom of God in the US which afforded men an opportunity to explore their own gender expectations and stereotypes. These tended to be little more than an opportunity for men to take time to bond with each other and celebrate their maleness together, having themselves felt excluded previously by female partners who appeared to have had such a good time doing *their* thing in women's groups. Rarely, if ever, does the issue of power ever come up for genuine debate and reconsideration.

This can apply even to individuals referred to as 'new' men. A new man spends more time with his children and willingly shares the day-to-day chores of parenthood but the values he models to his children are also relevant. Is he teaching them to be image-conscious, that only winning is good enough, that vulnerability is weak or that powerlessness means failure? Is he encouraging them to be sexual before their time? Is he helping them to be open and honest about their feelings? Does he share in the real shitwork in the home or leave it to his co-female parent?

What does the new father teach his sons? Is there coherence between the official line and informal behavior? Is he promoting suppression of fear and weakness, teaching them to use the weapon of aggression? Does he proclaim equality while rebuking his children's mother for her stupidity and incompetence? What language does he use to refer to women? What happens in the home is crucial for the formation of attitudes to gender because children will pick up any ambiguity, even if they don't have a word for it.

Often a man who professes to be keen to explore the softer sides of masculinity somehow still ends up ruling the roost, with a penchant, say, for pretty young girls or operating on the same old quasi-divine assumption that his word is final in any discussion. Sexism is not automatically voided when a man demonstrates a more 'feminine' side: this is a bit like assuming all gay men are sensitive sweeties who understand women far more than any straight man could. Men who enter the 'caring' professions of nursing, social work, counselling and therapy confound many women's naïve expectations that they will be any different in their sexist habits from bankers, builders or barmen. New men still take it for granted that they will head their own professional ladders. They play the same political games and are no less likely to dominate over women with their ideas, their language, their personalities and their egos. If there are changes, new men appear to want to remain on top and in control.

Fear of loss of power has been embedded in the foundation of masculine identity for thousands of years. Men don't like taking second place because competition is ingrained. However, reinventing oneself as a defence against the advances of feminism or agreeing to drop the excesses of chauvinist behavior while, at the same time, refusing to consider genuine power sharing is not taking responsibility but a response to fear.

Fears are fanned by occasional media reports of looming genetic irrelevance with forecasts of an eventual decline in the male species due to excess levels of oestrogen linked to male infertility: subconscious anxiety about the female coming into ascendance is guaranteed to raise a hackle or two. Anxiety is also increased when women renounce their own feminine qualities to become more like *them* – small wonder that men are susceptible to deep-seated fears of being ousted by women and afraid for their future.

So what am I hoping for? First, I hope that men will become more conscious of the issues involved. Obviously there is no single strategy: even within our own national culture, there are huge variations in male upbringing, in large part due to age, stage, religious faith and generational change. Men in their late twenties and thirties, for instance, have grown up with an agenda of equal right terminology embracing gender, race and sexual choice. They find it difficult to identify with traditional sexist or racist rhetoric and are somewhat baffled by the obvious hostility of others – especially older men – genuinely believing them to be wrong. The problem with this laidback approach is that they themselves often fail to see sexism playing out in many forms right under their noses. Older men, on the other hand, appear baffled about the whole issue of gender: do I say 'woman' or 'lady'? Shall I compliment her on her dress or will she find it offensive? Ascribing gender inequality to the era of the ark or focusing on superficial details both ignores current inequalities and allows a silence to be maintained which inevitably risks being collusive.

Nothing will change until men open their eyes, see the connections for themselves and then care enough to reconsider the whole system. Every man has a partner, daughter, girlfriend, sister, mother, aunt, grandmother or colleague who lives with sexism every single day of her life. Men don't see a lot of these implications because they don't experience them, and even if they do sense some inequality somewhere, personal discomfort, helplessness or plain cowardice are obstacles to real understanding.

Without seeing those connections, sexism will continue to flourish psychologically. It is pointless for a modern father to cheer on his daughter's newly found commitment to feminism while refusing to see that his own private habit of categorising women on a scale of attractiveness is in any way part of her problem; until he challenges his belief that, as man, he has an unquestionable right to be self-appointed judge of a woman's sexual viability, he will never begin to make the transition to a more humble stance of equality.

Genuinely coming to terms with one's own personal attitudes and assumptions really does require some humility. However, recognition of the depth and breadth of sexist conditioning is as important as sorting out your own personal agenda. A man cannot be raised without being exposed to the mindset of sexism and its manifestations. None of us is impervious. All we can do is acknowledge this and try to make different choices. I am not naïve enough to believe habits change easily but a vital step in changing any habit is to bring automatic assumptions and responses out of obscurity into the light where they can be scrutinised and discussed.

This means redefining feminism as an ideology which promotes the right to be accepted as a human being and not stifled by the accident of being born into a woman's body. Seeing the system in place and challenging it goes way beyond personal indignation at the behaviour of another man towards 'my wife' or 'my daughter' which is too closely linked to hierarchy and ownership. It is much more personally confronting to see that women are lower down the scale and more powerless because they are women. The catch is that this means all women; women who men consider attractive, gorgeous, ugly, miserable, tiresome, interesting, demanding, boring, cute, neurotic, sexy – the beauty and the bitch alike. This is in itself a fairly mind-blowing proposition.

Protest and challenge come in small but significant forms. It would be enormously significant were men to *speak up* and disagree with something that was being said or done; no big fight, just a gentle comment. Giving a voice to personal discomfort over particular assumptions or behaviour would break the harmful habit of silent collusion.

The next step: how does a man move from privately thinking and even publicly expressing that what happens is unfair or unfortunate to wanting to do something collectively about it? How can men be encouraged to come on board and fight alongside women who challenge institutional sexism and embedded social attitudes? Imagine how coherent legislation would make it impossible for employers to continue to get away with unequal pay without penalty. A seriously committed judicial review would improve the chances of rapists receiving sentences that reflected rape as a serious and unacceptable crime. Women's safety could be made a priority of expenditure instead of closing down the few police units dedicated to rape and domestic violence.

Imagine the major impact that collective action would have on women's safety in the world. Instead of being considered 'foolish' to travel alone at night or accused of getting herself into trouble, what would it be like to see a group of men emerge in any community who were determined to make their streets safe for women, not because women were weaker and in need of their protection but because women and girls deserved as equal human beings to be safe from harassment or assault?

Individually and collectively, a vital starting point for men's involvement is the future generation of men. Many children have grown into more tolerant adults regarding racial equality because of interracial educational experience. If boys cannot escape exposure to the assumption of permission to view and therefore treat a woman's body as an object, so much could be done while boys are young and impressionable. One way men could challenge unthinking sexism is to talk about it: bring it out into the open. Men could educate their sons or pupils; male celebrities could use their power to *challenge* sexist assumptions instead of conveying stereotypical predatory behavior as 'cool' which young male fans eagerly imitate. It appears that women are currently more alarmed by the high incidence of teenage boys watching pornography on their iPhones which is ironic: for what now should be obvious reasons, boys will identify more with and pay far more attention to their own gender than to women.

Apart from caring about the women they love, why should men bother to question sexism? If I wanted to present a logical argument, I could point out that sexism harms us all and demonstrate that gender stereotyping has an adverse effect on men as well. It is not uncommon for older men to have had to suppress a particular preference to follow what's expected of them by pursuing a career in industry or commerce or even just having to be the breadwinner in a family.

Pressures of gendered responsibility can have more fatal consequences. The suicide rate among men in Japan, for example, is very much higher than average. When a business fails or they are made redundant, men often feel unable to confide in their near and dear ones: shame of failure to meet the cultural expectations of being a man is carried to the extreme of suicide rather than being able to reach out as a human across the great chasm of gender rigidity.

In this country we are aware that young men – deeply traumatised by the experience of combat in war – are also victims of sexism. Even though there is now more acceptance of the legitimacy of PTSD, facilities are inadequate and little effective help is available. Furthermore, a request from a soldier for psychiatric help risks blocking his chances of promotion in the future: after all, emotion implies weakness and this is not what you want in a military man.

I could also argue that men suffer from being cut off from their emotions even though many simply don't register being out of touch with their innermost feelings. When reason rules and the significance of emotion in every area of life is trivialised as indulgence, there is not much incentive to learn more. Many men I've known and worked with have learned to become more attuned to their hearts only in response to some catalyst, an unexpected experience in life which has forced them to 'see' differently.

Among these catalysts have been a sudden ultimatum from a wife of thirty years who is threatening divorce because she is tired of lack of emotional connection; the illness or death of a loved one, the consequences of a serious accident or disease and exposure to one's own or another's extreme vulnerability. Trauma offers an opportunity to reassess normal preoccupations and personal behaviour through the experience of suffering.

Ultimately, though, this isn't about rational arguments. Taking feminism seriously means understanding the consequences of sexism both intellectually and emotionally: opening the heart to allow another dimension of being into consciousness, the human being inside the gendered body.

13
A RELATIONSHIP OF EQUALS

Men need to help and guide each other through change but change will only be effective if emotion is included. Men often fear *fear* itself but deeper down there may be emotions of grief and rage at their own oppression within a sexist system.

One major challenge will be dismantling the widespread belief that a sexually-aroused male will suffer devastating consequences should his erection not be sucked or fucked or coaxed into ejaculation. This assumption has in no way diminished with modern sexual permissiveness. As long as this belief remains uncontested, it will remain as a pivotal point of inequality (and power over women) in any heterosexual interaction.

Is it possible to celebrate male procreativity without the relentless linear emphasis on sexual mechanics and performance? Can sexual arousal occur without making the other into an 'object of desire'? Can lust live alongside love? A patriarchal mentality has taught many men to sever the link between heart and penis – is it possible to reconnect? Is it possible for us to revisualise the body not as a set of connected fragments but as an integrated whole? I don't know the answers but if men believe they too stand to gain from increased humanity rather than increased stereotypical masculinity then we can begin a dialogue.

Women cannot make this transition for men because they have their own battles to fight. Too many women opt for keeping quiet, allowing their own needs and feelings to be discounted; too many women stay in loveless relationships and hold back from being true to themselves, all through fear of being alone. Instead of being hampered by self-doubt women have to find some authentic power within, having spent too long surviving on the vicarious experience of power – being like men or liked by men – to compensate for a lack of emotional autonomy.

An experience of equal power would make all the difference but, until that develops, care and love for others is easily distorted while women continue to relate to others as if they possessed no inner autonomy at all. From the first questions I ask in an assertiveness class – What is it that *you* want? What do *you* feel? How do *you* respond? What do *you* experience? – it is very clear that a strong, flexible and certain sense of self is suffocating under an intense preoccupation with how one is seen or might appear to others. Women's sensitivity to *others'* needs, feelings, reactions and problems does not stem automatically from a sense of equality or a balance between self and other. It stems from a life of being vigilant. This is a vigilance arising as much from insecurity as love.

If it were based more in love, there would be a felt equality between self and other, a balance between 'what I want' and 'what you want', between 'your needs' and 'my needs'. Without equality, care and concern become entangled with the essential role of defining ourselves.

A RELATIONSHIP OF EQUALS

Perhaps a woman's greatest challenge is to stop deriding her nature as a fundamental flaw. Discovering and appreciating the beauty of her body and her bodily processes would not only help her stand alone in her own power but also make her see that a woman's power is not poison – it is a necessary medicine in today's world.

In the face of the immense challenge to both genders, there is one particular dimension of being human which gives me hope: our capacity for friendship. A little more love between the sexes would not go amiss. I don't mean 'lurve' (as in Mills & Boon) and I don't mean 'luv' which one professes to feel instantly for everybody (as long as it demands absolutely no effort). I mean the kind of love associated with friendship. This is because friendship is essentially equal; in fact, it is only possible between equals.

My own experience of friendship is that differences of age, status, education, outlook, experience, background are subsumed by an overarching care, a joint interest, a liking, a respect, a trust and a willingness to be oneself, an ability to get things wrong, be vulnerable, to challenge and be challenged. Friendship assumes individuality and togetherness at the same time: you can be angry, loving, affectionate, reach out in compassion or in sorrow and you can be truthful. Your friend wants the best for you, listens to all of you, accepting your contradictions and faults as part of you; you feel heard, seen for who you are rather than what you are expected to be. You take risks and weather hard times together because your friendship is worth sustaining.

Friendships do not thrive on mistrust or walking on eggshells. Friendship is not based on someone being your 'other half', being an object onto whom you can project all your fantasies or needs. Friendship is not someone playing Jack to your Jill (or *vice versa*), when the other becomes a mere yardstick against which to measure your own gender potential or lack of it. Friendship offers an effective antidote to sexism: the masculine/feminine quotient does not have to dominate as the sole model for hetero- or homosexual relationships.

As long as it is unchallenged, sexism will continue to erode genuine respect between men and women. Respect can come from mutuality which is impossible in an unequal system; respect can also be elicited by someone above you if you can honestly acknowledge that they have abilities, qualities, skills or experience that amply justifies the higher position. How can women truly respect men when their 'higher' position is based on nothing but the chance event of being born with testicles?

An emphasis on friendship between men and women – as a basis for a sexual relationship – would help build respect. In addition it would help diminish the tendency to see women's bodies as objects: if men loved women as equal human beings, as subjects in their own right, they could not objectify them so easily in their minds.

Love cancels out the vision of the other as object; as soon as you stop relating to a body – someone else's or your own – as an object, you see and feel differently. Love allows the heart to open in a way that sees through the external trappings to the person residing within. This is the ultimate goal of feminism: to see beyond gender to the whole person.

14
OUR GENDERED PLANET

During the months of working on this book, I've ended up in many impromptu discussions as a result of being asked what I'm currently writing about. What always seems to happen is that after a short while, the conversation widens out from gender issues to a much broader frame of reference: bullying, terrorism, drones, disrespect for others, appalling treatment of the elderly as objects, corruption, the stranglehold of corporations on politics, the lies we are told in the media and so on. As the feeling of hopelessness and helplessness takes over, the conversation usually stutters to an end.

I've witnessed this several times now and it strikes me that we have some underlying awareness that we live in a gendered world and that many of us do not like what we see. We inhabit a world imbalanced by one particular way of seeing, being and behaving. For a start, the staggering inequality between upper and lower layers of society in every nation is a direct consequence of patriarchal formulation. Even though we are informed authoritatively that inequality is not good for humanity – physically, psychologically and socially – we live today with more extremes of inequality of wealth and access to many vital resources than ever before in the history of our planet.

OUR GENDERED PLANET

Every now and then someone makes an oblique reference to how it might be different if women figured more prominently in the world. Christine la Garde, for instance, has suggested that more women economists would have prevented the excessive risks that triggered the global economic collapse in 2008; Aung San Suu Kyi has been quoted as saying, 'The education of and empowerment of women throughout the world cannot fail to result in a more caring, tolerant, just and peaceful life for all.' What exactly are these women implying?

Both of them allude to gender difference, to intrinsic qualities in the female which have become eclipsed by the glaring lights of patriarchal dogma. Any reference to gender stereotypes is now suspect in a post-modern climate, but nevertheless, all stereotypes contain an element of truth. I believe that women's bodies allow for a different experience of the world. In pagan cultures, it used to be completely accepted that women possess a natural ability to summon up the energies and powers of the elements, that women are naturally more connected to the earth. Women potentially have a sense of what is called 'interiority' that many men miss out on. Female bodies offer a different experience of life: not more or less important but different. If envy hadn't trumped the spirit of co-operation, things might have been a lot different today.

In all the years I have worked with women, I have found that an awareness of the 'other' is almost always present. Sometimes this overlaps with instinctual caring tendencies: sensitivity to changes in mood, to suffering, to unspoken needs. Generally speaking, women pick up emotional signals more readily; their emotional antennae are more sensitised to tension and distress; women are inclined towards reconciliation rather than conflict, demonstrating an urge to communicate rather than to shut off in silence. Women are capable of going to extraordinary lengths of planning and preparation to give pleasure to someone they care for; taking trouble with choice of gifts, remembering birthdays and anniversaries. This is an aspect of life that women often excel at though obviously it is not considered an important contribution, like making money, waging war or solving political crises. Nevertheless, it is these small things which oil the wheels of relationship.

I have no way of knowing for sure whether women, any more than men, have an innate sensitivity or tenderness towards others. Recent research in US in fact suggests that the genders are not so fundamentally differently from each other biologically. The need to survive in the muted group cannot be taken completely out of the picture in that we learn to watch and look out more, to monitor and read signs. Whatever the mix of nature and conditioning, though, it is a definite strength many women manifest: a strong awareness of relationship/context/other/emotion.

The tendency to emulate rather than innovate means women have failed so far to introduce different values into the workplace, the home or society in general. For all the comments about what a difference it would make if women contributed more equally, we are unlikely to have the chance to see any potential realised: qualities which could make a real difference to all of us will be forever held in check until women see themselves as humans of equal stature.

Equality of opportunity has to be substantive. The repercussions of the 'safety gap' I referred to earlier are not restricted to travelling alone at night. The lack of internal security – as a constant experience – affects many women in situations in which they do not feel 'at home': when they are at odds with behaviour that's expected of them, whenever they are fearful of an aggressive response or anticipate a hostile reaction or adverse criticism. It is a generally acknowledged fact that the experience of anxiety and insecurity will restrict any person's ability to contribute, initiate, challenge, be creative or collaborate fully with others. So it's probably worth remembering that equality will only be achieved when women feel more security from the outside and genuine self-confidence on the inside: a self-confidence that derives from being true to oneself, not being compelled to live every aspect of life according to others' rules. Then equality of opportunity might have some real meaning in the workplace and every other sphere of life.

This requires men to be open to the possibility of another way of viewing the world. It also requires men to relinquish some of their habitual power and overcome their knee-jerk resistance to learning from women, to being led by women and to allowing women's voices, their authentic voices to be heard.

Without getting into fantasies (or nightmares!) about what would happen if women ruled the world, consider the impact that gender equality might have. Experts have already stated that problems of hunger and malnutrition in the world will not be solved without first addressing specific gender inequalities concerning rights to ownership of farming land.

Imagine what else might be different if there was substantive and material equality of contribution to the overseeing of our planet; if women went beyond a merely reactive to a proactive role in establishing an alternative to balance the exclusive model currently running the show.

Perhaps the value of relationship would be regarded as important as the ubiquitous business model of transaction. The obsession with linear goals might be tempered by consideration of impact on others; the tendency to segregate and exclude might be balanced by openness to accommodation and inclusiveness; concepts of mental health, education and intelligence might no longer be considered in relation to one dominant norm but contextualised and multi-faceted. War might even become unseated from its premier position as the first choice of response to conflict; maybe men would be willing to talk together instead of fighting each other, to accommodate rather than eliminate.

Instead of a world increasingly controlled by large and small inanimate machines, operated by complex systems of data units where quantity and speed are paramount, there might also be an equivalent emphasis on human potential. The need to prioritise the quality of relationship, physical contact, community and meaningful communication –

aspects of human life which require time and sustained effort – might be ascribed equal importance alongside numerical targets and objectives. Perhaps the vulnerability of the mentally ill, the elderly, the young, the infirm, the have-nots of society would be approached with compassion instead of contempt. We might even revive the virtue of gentleness.

Maybe the meaning of nature would resonate with a deeper significance than an advertising concept to sell soup or shampoo. Many feminists have pointed to the patriarchal connection between our psychological and physical approach to nature and the objectification of the female body. It's pretty obvious that 'Mother Nature' is both admired for her beauty and feared for her power. It's also easy to find an awful lot of evidence of treating the natural world as an object: to be plundered, used, fracked, cracked, drilled, penetrated, poisoned, violated and utterly exhausted for man's own 'superior' needs.

The imperative to conquer nature might be replaced with a sense of reverence. Many writers – theologians, ecologists, ecological feminists, poets and scientists – have written of the urgent need for a new attitude to the environment. The creation-centred vision of man as superior to nature might be balanced by the alternative of man as one part of nature.

More frivolous fantasies extend to complementing the phallocratic legacy of the past with some woman-centred symbols. Three thousand years of ubiquitous columns, towers, obelisks and spires might be augmented by symbols of caverns, wombs and circles as found in Neolithic tombs. Who knows? At this stage, one can really only imagine.

I have written this book in the hope that understanding, truly understanding the significance of feminism will persuade men to declare themselves openly against sexism. First, unconscious habits have to be nudged into consciousness: assumptions questioned, connections made, unthinking sexism transformed into thinking sexism. Awareness precedes any possible consideration of change.

Then we have to *care* enough to want to change. After sixty years on this planet – as a woman – my conclusion is that sexism is a truly hideous system. I have always found that, as a mindset, sexism has the infallible knack of taking something ordinary, even beautiful, and distorting it into something fearsome and ugly. Its over-riding legacy is aggression. The value of the emotion of anger as a force for change has been smothered by lifelong conditioning in aggression; an ever-present response to fear of powerlessness, actively militating against equality.

Patriarchally-skewed perceptions turn friends into enemies; reduce the fundamental beauty and integrity of the human body into an object to be controlled; pervert a child's innocence into a vehicle for sexual gratification; and, instead of inspiring awe, reduce the natural environment to a dispensable irrelevance. Women are prevented from appreciating the beauty of their own bodies and from exercising their own authentic power. Men's resources for tenderness and devotion (especially to other men) remain largely untapped.

Although sexism may have shaped life as we know it, we need to recognise once and for all that it is *not* part of our human biological imperative like needing oxygen or water to maintain life on this planet. It is part of a system which has lasted a very long time but it is nevertheless possible to turn a psychological switch and see differently. After all, the energy needed for any creative action to improve our world needs us *all* to contribute.

I shall end where I began, with a few men's statements about racism on the football pitch – statements which gave me the idea for this book. As I listened then, I found myself imagining what it would be like to hear those men say with equal vehemence 'we should not tolerate sexism in this day and age' or 'we must adopt a zero-tolerance approach to sexism in all its forms' or even hearing men assert that 'sexism brings shame on humanity for all of us'. Now that's something to hope for!

MORE FROM THE AUTHOR

Praise for the million-selling *A Woman in Your Own Right* (ISBN 9780704372696, £10), first published in 1982 and today considered the core study on assertiveness:

'In creating a thirtieth anniversary edition of her groundbreaking book on assertiveness *A Woman in Your Own Right*, Anne Dickson has been adroit in understanding how the shift in social and political changes affecting women have meant that assertiveness is too often re-interpreted as about being the toughest gal on the block, and to hell with sisterhood. Yet underneath this veneer, for all the changes there have been, younger women find it as difficult as ever to be comfortably assertive, or to feel good with themselves in our image-led culture. In this new version Dickson has skilfully re-assessed what guidance is needed in a social context so altered in three decades. It is a book at least as important as it ever was'

Angela Neustatter

'Anne Dickson's book is the bible for anyone who wants to stand on their own two feet, look life in the eye and get their voice heard. Thirty years on I still find the skills taught in its pages to be invaluable on a daily basis'

Lesley Garner

'*A Woman in Your Own Right* explores the misery and frustration which can arise from compliance with traditional ideas about a woman's role...convincing you that you have the power to make choices and be your own person'

Company

'Assertiveness leaves you with a tremendous feeling of self-confidence, self-respect, self-worth. The freedom to be who you are, not who other people think you are'

Cosmopolitan

REVISED
30TH ANNIVERSARY
EDITION

A WOMAN

IN YOUR

OWN RIGHT

ASSERTIVENESS AND YOU

Anne Dickson